Welcome to
ENTREPRENEUR
COUNTRY

Welcome to
ENTREPRENEUR COUNTRY

WHAT IT IS
HOW TO FIND IT
WHY YOU SHOULD GO THERE

Julie Meyer

CONSTABLE • LONDON

Constable & Robinson Ltd
55–56 Russell Square
London WC1B 4HP
www.constablerobinson.com

First published in the UK by Constable,
an imprint of Constable & Robinson Ltd, 2012

A copy of the British Library Cataloguing in
Publication Data is available from the British Library

ISBN: 978-1-78033-894-1 (hardback)
ISBN: 978-1-78033-896-5 (ebook)

Printed and bound in the UK

1 3 5 7 9 10 8 6 4 2

Image on page 109 courtesy of ShutterStock.

CONTENTS

For David ... Everywhere

This book is for those of you who go every day.

I am convinced that we are *all* going to go to Entrepreneur Country. Some of us are aware of its existence from friends, books, movies and chatter. Some of us go there daily: you can see it in our wrinkles, our laugh lines, our furrowed brows. Some of us will, but just don't know it yet. Some of us are scared of it, but that fear is really a fear of something else inside of us. Some of us are considering going there, but have to convince our families first. Some of us can help others get there faster. Some of us can make it a really great place. Our children, however, will all grow up there.

All of us are going to Entrepreneur Country. It takes its citizens not by cultural background, wealth, class or intelligence. It values ingenuity, hard work, collaboration and passion.

This is bottom up. This isn't top down.

Each of us has a role to play in Entrepreneur Country. It's tied to how we make the country operate best. Citizens of Entrepreneur Country don't have the luxury of just working nine to five, then going home and locking the door.

As in all transformational movements throughout history, the winners are those who get to the other side first.

Welcome then – to Entrepreneur Country.

INTRODUCTION

So there I was. Eight o'clock on a Friday morning at the advisory board meeting of a prestigious national business awards programme in London. I had been asked to lead the nominations and judging panel for the entrepreneurship category. The twenty-member board was being asked for its recommendations over coffee and croissants, with the goal to make this awards programme stand out from all the others that had sprung up over the past decade.

I listened as the BBC's representative suggested that we should have a 'public services' category. After all, he said, HM Revenue and Customs had secured two prominent business awards the previous year. I scratched my head and said, 'If we really have to give a "public service" award, it should simply be for the body that has lived within its budget and provided the most efficiency – the one that has done more with less in real terms. But public services aren't in fact businesses, so why consider them for business awards?'

Silence.

I described how the Entrepreneurship Award could be developed and mentioned some recent research from NESTA, the UK's Innovation Agency: 'Only six per cent of all UK businesses are defined as "high growth", but they create fifty-four per cent of all new jobs for the nation.'

From the other side of the table, the chairman of a major UK PLC interrupted with a loud cough. He pushed his glasses to the end of his nose, studiously refused to look at me, and said, 'Well, I'm a business person [with the implication clearly being that I could not possibly be] and I know that that is categorically untrue.'

Looking directly at him, though he still avoided my eyes, I said, 'They don't make up these reports. NESTA has done its research twice and it keeps finding the same results.'

Silence.

I suddenly felt very alone in the room. Nevertheless, I sat up straight and just kept looking at him not looking at me. We were meant to be creating an awards programme that would honour the nation's great businesses. We should have been singing from the same hymn sheet. As far as I was concerned, the whole point of the exercise was to showcase the businesses that were becoming major players. But that morning, in that room, there seemed to be a fundamental lack of understanding as to who is driving the train of economic growth. It's not big business. It's not the public sector. High-growth small and medium enterprises (SMEs) *are* economic policy in the UK. They are not just elements of it; they are at the heart of it. We should be focusing on, and celebrating, the 'vital 6 per cent'.

This was blindingly obvious to me, so I started to wonder why a leading journalist and the chairman of one of the UK's largest companies couldn't see it. Hadn't he read NESTA's report? Or was it just arrogance?

No. It just wasn't in his interest to accept that the 'vital 6 per cent' now drive Britain's economy.

Or so he thought.

At that moment, I realised the crucial difference between us. Every day I deal with the enormous pressures and the tremendous delights of running my own business. And I hang out with other entrepreneurs, managing directors, and small-business owners who are doing exactly the same thing. We finish every day thoroughly exhausted, but it's a good kind of exhaustion – the sort you feel

13

after running a marathon. Every day we learn new things and accomplish more than we ever thought possible. Every day those around us surprise us with their resilience, their commitment, their passion, their insight, and their desire to be part of something greater than themselves. We work in an environment that values ingenuity, hard work, collaboration and passion. The old divisions of cultural background, wealth and class have no part to play here.

We go to a different country every day – *Entrepreneur Country* – and we are citizens of that place.

Others are aware of its existence but have not yet taken the plunge and stepped inside. Some of them are scared; others can't wait to join us but need to convince their families that it is the right thing to do. We can encourage them, help them get here faster and make it an even better place than it is already. But in the future, *everyone* will make the journey and live in Entrepreneur Country. Our children will grow up here.

Work is hard in Entrepreneur Country: you can see it in our wrinkles, our laugh lines, our furrowed brows. We don't have the luxury of working nine to five, then going home and locking the door. Instead, we drink far too much coffee and work seventy to ninety-hour weeks. Each and every day we have to deal with:

➤ Customers not paying on time.

➤ Delays of product launches.

➤ Unsympathetic and condescending bank managers.

➤ Employees who are only visiting Entrepreneur Country and would really rather be somewhere else.

➤ The inept or even Kafkaesque machinations of HMRC.

➤ The media, who lazily lump us in with bankers who have never risked a penny of their own money.

➤ And venture capitalists who forget that they should be in the business of helping entrepreneurs maximise their potential.

Nevertheless, I drive the train.

And what is the reward for all of this hard work and hassle? Often not much, at least initially. Most entrepreneurs and business owners are broke for years. One couple I know who run a business services firm maxed out *ninety-two* credit cards and eventually lost their home. I'm not applauding this – just observing that it happens. They are currently fighting their way back, and I give them a fifty/fifty chance of making it. They are good people, and have guided a large swath of the UK's SMEs through the digital landscape. Most importantly, they are happy. Like

15

all the other citizens of Entrepreneur Country, they are determined to keep driving their own train.

I've always dreamed of driving the train actually. I knew I wasn't good at repairing the tracks or designing the interiors of the coaches. But I do have a really good sense of direction and I'm fearless, indefatigable. I don't get a second wind each day. I get fifteen. I'm also not afraid to change direction if it will help me reach my final destination.

Day in, day out, it's my job to keep the train on track. Sure, there are moments when it looks as if it might derail, but I've always survived those near-death experiences somehow – mostly by fighting the right battles, having a sixth contingency plan for when the first five fail, building relationships with guardian angels early, and picking the best people for my team. The train drivers in Entrepreneur Country do not necessarily have big company or college backgrounds, and they certainly do not all pay themselves fat base salaries, but they know how to make things happen and keep their teams happy. Then they get up and do it all over again. Day after day.

Fortunately, there are plenty of other train drivers in Entrepreneur Country, and they're usually willing to help us understand whatever we don't know. Then we return the favour. We all wear a similar expression: stressed, maybe not happy, but definitely optimistic. Every day, we pull on that optimism like a coat to shield us from the cold. Eventually, the breakthrough moment will come and all the near misses will be forgotten as we celebrate reaching our destination. That is what binds all of the drivers together.

Whether we are housewives-turned-kitchen-table-entrepreneurs in Devon, B&B owners in Brighton, independent production companies in Manchester, Avon's thousands of micro-entrepreneurs, university students in Newcastle, Cambridge scientists, Silicon Valley geeks in a garage, Swedish digital pirates or Israeli fighter-pilots-turned-tech-entrepreneurs, we all know that entrepreneurship and business ownership are asymmetrical.

We are Davids in a world of Goliaths: we are small, but we will win in the end. There's no question about it. A number of plodding Goliaths might be heading in the same direction, some might even step on the tracks to block our path, but our trains are moving faster and with greater purpose than any Goliath could ever understand. Goliaths continue to underestimate each and every David. They assume that he will come flying off the tracks at the next junction or slam into the buffers at the next station.

But David wins. David with his slingshot wins. And Goliath scratches his head, and can't figure out for the life of him how he does it.

LinkedIn went public in early 2011 with a multi-billion-dollar valuation.

But it began as a 'David', and had to make its way through the treacherous early years of being the little guy. Like most successful firms, the company's success was far from assured, and there were many perilous experiences along the way. It's just that no one talks about them now; it's not always fun to relive near-death experiences.

David knows that one false move, one unexpected event, and he's out. No one will notice or care about your demise.

So, David never relaxes. He never really exhales. He just keeps driving the train each and every day. But he does not have to compete with the Goliaths entirely on his own. He can bring others on board to run the catering car, collect the tickets, even work on the engine and make the train run faster.

The train is only as strong as its weakest component, but David doesn't need to get involved with every problem that develops. He's not a dictator; he's just the driver. A lot of people on the train know much more than he does about precisely what's happening in every carriage. They feed all of that knowledge into the route map, but they don't necessarily want to be up front with their hands on the controls. Many of them know that they would not enjoy the pressure that comes with driving the train. And yet, whatever they do is more than just a job to them. They are committed to maintaining the momentum of the train. They want to win. And they will do everything in their power to make that happen.

Of course, the journey through Entrepreneur Country is not always entirely smooth:

➤ Some of the staff panic whenever the train judders over track that hasn't been properly maintained because of cash-flow problems.

➤ Others feel queasy every time the train heads off in a new direction at great speed and wish that David the driver would occasionally slow down a little.

➤ Others seemed happy to board the train but now keep asking, 'Where's first class? What do you mean there's no first class? I was looking for an easy life, not a fast train. How do I get off?'

➤ Sometimes fuel costs rise and David has to make the tough decision to cut several carriages to compensate.

At each station, we see familiar faces – friends, family, former colleagues – who consider getting on. They wave and smile. They act as if it's their choice when they get on. It's not. *This train is coming to you.* Some of them jump on board. Many do not. They might admire the train as it heads off towards the distant horizon, but they would rather stay in their big country houses with an early-evening glass of Pinot Grigio watching the sun set. They sense that boarding the train might disturb their cherished work–life balance. (They're quite right about that!) But now they have missed this opportunity to get on the train, and it's unclear whether they will be able to find quite such a good seat the next time it pulls into their station.

Meanwhile, we just keep going. 'We've never had it so good,' we tell ourselves to help us through the difficult times. Despite all of the money worries and the long hours, we love the freedom. We feel alive.

And we recognise that we are obsessed. This doesn't feel abnormal to us.

But it is.

Alastair Lukies, the CEO of Monitise, the global leader in the field of mobile money, texted me one Friday night in 2006: '102 meetings, 67 nights away from my wife, but we got the deal. We have a client.' Few people will view that as rational behaviour. No one 'normal' goes to 102 meetings to win a single client. Only an obsessed entrepreneur who ends up changing the world does that.

Even those people who don't understand how vital the 6 per cent is – and it is, or those who want to treat public services as businesses – which they are not, all of the people in the countryside too – they all benefit from our obsession and from the fact that we are willing to live such abnormal lives. Driving the train, carrying the freight, paying the tolls, staying on track, putting in the hard miles, emerging from a series of tunnels, picking up other bloodied and busted Davids whose own trains have derailed, dusting them down and giving them a chance to recuperate in the back of the train. Then, finally, reaching our destination.

***

Entrepreneur Country can be a series of episodes that you live. At the moment, you might not consider yourself a citizen of Entrepreneur Country, but think about the ways in which society is changing:

➤ Your next-door neighbour is now running his own e-commerce business from home.

➤ You read one too many newspaper articles about waste in government and feel that something really radical should be done about it. More to the point, you have an idea about what that 'something' should be.

➤ Your thirteen-year-old daughter is obsessed with setting up her own fashion label.

➤ Your mother blogs daily about her life, and what she's writing is rather thought-provoking.

➤ You don't know anyone under the age of thirty who thinks they work for someone else any more.

➤ Your seven-year-old son asked the other day, 'What do

we need politicians for?' and you were unable to give him an answer.

➤ You read somewhere that it took seventy-eight years for the television to be adopted by 150 million users, fifty-four years for the fixed-line telephone to reach the same number, thirty-four years for the fax, seventeen years for the mobile phone, and only five years for Facebook. You can see where this is going ...

➤ You stopped watching television years ago, and have developed an odd fascination with reading and posting on Wikipedia and watching YouTube videos.

➤ Your cousin, who went bankrupt a few years ago, is now running a thriving training business.

➤ Your natural gift for 'thinking of the group' instead of just your own small patch seems to be becoming more relevant.

➤ You stopped worrying about being discriminated against because you are a woman/from an ethnic minority/over fifty/disabled, and have shifted into a different mode. It's not that the discrimination doesn't matter. Of course it does. It's just that you are too consumed with what you are doing to be upset about it. You'd rather focus on being a great role model and changing the world.

➤ Your neighbourhood has started campaigning for the local council to post its full accounts online to ensure total transparency of spending and receipts.

You don't initially see them as a new landscape until you

get on the train, and observe the difference from the countryside outside and the order of the train inside.

It all makes sense backwards.

You don't initially connect the dots. Until you do. The dots become a line; the line becomes a track. The train flies past.

Eventually you see that how society organises itself is changing. This is more than just a job. Your whole psyche is engaged. The neighbourhood is different – not just the office. The train is picking up speed and keeps coming around the stations more frequently.

➤ You find yourself thinking about the train *all the time*.

➤ You don't want to spend time with people you don't like any more.

➤ You refuse to waste your time watching bad TV again.

➤ You can't wait to get out of bed in the morning.

➤ You figure out within fifteen minutes of talking to someone new whether they believe the same things you believe. And you don't remember where this idea of believing emerged from. You find yourself saying, 'I believe...'

24   It must be that train ... must be Entrepreneur Country.

It feels like an act of faith getting on that train. You keep looking at the door as you think about stepping on to it. You have a sense of erasing a lot of what doesn't work in life by getting on board. But it's far from certain exactly what will happen next.

Silence.

I know which side of history I want to be on.

Do you?

CHAPTER 1

CAPITAL FOLLOWS IDEAS

Picture the scene: you are twenty-three years old, you are living in a foreign country and you have little money. You have to figure out a way to earn a living. What do you do?

You set up your own one-man business managing training programmes for corporates. It is small, but it teaches you valuable lessons for the future.

Now, fast forward eight years. Your day job is making investments at the height of the dot-com boom, but you are devoting more and more of your free time to managing the spontaneous explosion of interest in a network of entrepreneurs that you run. Your gut tells you that this 'side' business – which you have called First Tuesday (because the networking events happen on the first Tuesday of the month) – could be very big. You take the biggest risk of your life and quit your job with the £35,000 bonus cheque from your employer as your cushion. You take First Tuesday to forty-five cities around the world and attract 500,000 members. A leading venture capitalist offers to invest $1 million in your burgeoning network, which is still headquartered in your living room. One year later, you sell First Tuesday for $50 million.

The network's viral growth and exit are staggering. You almost can't keep up with it. You started with nothing but an idea. Your idea. But you worked 24/7 for twenty-one months ... and the capital found you.

***

I lived in Paris from September 1988 to June 1993. When I arrived, I had just graduated from Valparaiso University, near Chicago, with an English and Humanities honours degree. I had also studied French, but my spoken French was *un échec total* (a total failure). I was humbled but determined: I would learn the language. So off I went to Paris two months after graduation. Although I was focused on learning to speak French, what I actually learned during my time in France was how to make my own way in the world.

Not surprisingly, France was not waiting for me with open arms.

I showed up knowing no one, and I didn't really have a plan of action other than a wild exploration of everything French. I came from a comfortable,

27

safe and secure family background, but I knew that I still had to figure out who I was – apart from and in connection to the family values that my parents had instilled in me. It was this that drove me to get on that plane and fly to Paris. I wanted to learn what my unique contribution to the world would be. Also, I didn't want to be the 'baby' of the family for ever.

One of the first things I discovered was what I initially interpreted as stubborn French negativity. Whereas Americans say 'yes' to almost everything, because they are a naturally optimistic people, the first reaction of the French to most things is *'non'*. At first, I couldn't understand why they were always so negative, but soon I came to realise that it was because they negotiate everything. That *'non'* is their way of saying: 'Prove to me how badly you want this.' Once I figured that out, France toughened me up and made me hugely resourceful. I wouldn't let the bastards get me down. I had no home court advantage in Paris. No one in my family had any connections to Paris. I showed up knowing no one, and I didn't really have a plan other than to learn French and to figure out who I was.

By teaching English to French executives at Hewlett-Packard, 3Com and other technology firms, I started to understand how technology was changing the world. The micro-computer was on the rise, and computing was transforming enterprises. I morphed my language teaching into consulting on marketing and cross-cultural issues, and secured consulting jobs at the OECD and elsewhere. But overall, I was still frustrated. The world was big and I was small – without a real plan – and I didn't know how to change that.

Then my boyfriend said something that changed my life for ever. He said, 'Don't worry about money, Julie. Don't do something because you have or don't have the money. If you are good at it, clear about your goals, convincing in the execution, the money will find you.' The impact of what he said went deep. He realised that my focus was on worrying about money rather than concentrating on building my expertise. I thought he was being ridiculous when I heard him say that, and I was cool towards him for the rest of the weekend. 'Easy for you to say,' I thought. 'You're successful, older, respected.' Then I realised that that was the point. He was successful, older, respected.

So, straight out of university, I got on that plane in September 1998 to go to Paris to 'find myself'.

What would my unique contribution to the world be?

➤ I really didn't have that much money to start off with. I worked like crazy to give English lessons, and at one point had sixty-five students within Hewlett-Packard France.

➤ But I kept asking myself how was I going to break
  through to the next level?

➤ I couldn't see myself doing the odd modelling job,
  teaching English, and dating French men for ever.

The problem was that I was too focused on the money.
And I should have been developing my ideas, my
expertise, and my strengths. It just always seemed that
everything came back to money, and my relative lack
of it.

I was not able to really break through until I went
to INSEAD, a European business school based in
Fontainebleau, France in 1997 at age thirty. Confronted
with 220 other students who all also had fitted the profile
to be selected, I came across people who were so much
better at certain business domains than I would ever be.
Nevertheless, I started to discover in those amphitheatres
in Fontainebleau, France where my own strengths lay:

➤ At twenty-three I knew the thrill and terror of working
  for myself in a foreign country.

➤ I had managed people from a young age, which many
  of my INSEAD classmates hadn't, gaining experience
  hiring and firing from age twenty-five.

➤ I was a macro and lateral thinker, a hard worker and an
  optimistic spirit.

➤ I had always had empathy for the underdog, but hadn't seen it as a strength.

➤ I started to realise that I usually connected with the CEO of any company I met. I would find myself in situations with people who had much more responsibility than I did, and found that it was easier to talk to them than it was talking to the people who reported to them. Again, I hadn't understood why this happened – only that it did.

➤ Marketing and communications came naturally to me.

➤ I also could see that I had a high risk threshold. Things that I would bite off seemed to either horrify or scare my classmates. I just assumed I'd figure things out.

➤ Slowly I realised that I was building a high level of confidence in my ability to take the risk out of opportunities in unstructured situations, creating frameworks and systems as I would work through an opportunity.

➤ Most importantly, though, I realised I was really happy being on my own. Not all the time, mind you, but I didn't crave time with people; I craved time on my own to think and execute my plans. I was an introvert – one with a passionate mission in mind, but an introvert none the less. I gathered steam on my own. My batteries would deplete in groups, and I would have to recharge by having 'Julie time' just on my own. I had thought of that too as a weakness or an oddity growing up, but realised that it gave me great freedom as an adult.

➤ Through some of the peculiarities of my childhood, I had become quite independent at an early age.

➤ Throughout my life, I have always been willing to defuse the bombs whereas most people want to wait to see that everything is safe before they pick them up.

In short, I had the makings of a young David.

But even as I was developing my abilities with my slingshot, I was still – more frequently than not – forgetting what happened to Goliath in the end. I was still thinking too much about me, and not realising that others had weaknesses too.

> It has been my experience over the past twenty years, that the money does find you. You have to have an almighty idea. You have to be convincing. You must have done your homework. You must sacrifice a 'normal life'. You must work hard. And you must never give up, accept 'no', or go away – even when 'they' want you to. But the money *does* find you.

So, I believe that capital follows ideas. It always has, and always will.

If we look throughout history at people who have changed the game for the epoch in which they lived, they typically were backed by financiers, families or royalty, who put them on retainer, or funded their work – sometimes to ensure that no one else would back them.

The rivalry of Leonardo Da Vinci and Michelangelo 500 years ago was over who would secure the most prestigious commissions from the most influential patrons. The men of the establishment – whether Borgias or the Medici family – wanted to fund the discoveries of art, medicine and travel.

Christopher Columbus may be remembered for his discovery of the Americas, but Queen Isabella took him out of the market by having him work for her.

Read up on the Rothschilds, the Warburgs and any other banking dynasty, and you will see through the lines a quest to fund the industrial giants of the day.

Entrepreneurs are the contemporary equivalents. They are the purveyors of ideas, which they apply to the market and from which they create businesses. Financiers back them in order to seal the best grip on the economic rights to those ideas. From Sand Hill Road, the road in Silicon Valley where all of the major venture capitalists are located, to Mayfair, from the Cambridge tech cluster to the thousands of garages every place where entrepreneurs start to concoct the new new thing, people change the world with their ideas about how the world *should* work. Money merely flows to the best ideas and people for the best return. It doesn't start the party; the entrepreneur does that.

Money is a utility to achieve something. It is nothing more than a means to achieve an end. It shouldn't be a goal in itself.

The financial services industry has ignored this golden rule over the past couple of decades and has become a massively complex industry in its own right, which contributed to the financial crisis of 2008–2011. The financial services industry should simply be a service industry for industry, with responsibility for:

➤ **The backing of digital industrialists.**

➤ **The facilitation of corporate transactions.**

➤ **The development of new growth areas for business.**

➤ **The enablement of better lives.**

When actions are divorced from the outcomes they create, problems arise. Alignment towards the betterment of industry must be the goal. The worship of finance for finance's sake, for the sake of bonuses, or for the tax revenue, won't grow the real economy of retailers, manufacturers, entrepreneurs and technologists. Financiers should measure themselves by the sustainable outcomes that business and industry are able to generate through the use of financial services.

One of the key reasons that Europe doesn't have as many Facebooks, Apples, Amazons and Googles as the US is that those in the business of the financing of entrepreneurship still don't:

➤ **understand the entrepreneur in all his or her obsession – not having been David themselves, they have an implicit mistrust and desire to control David;**

➤ **see him/her as the creator of value;**

➤ **recognise that he/she is the hero.**

So, I say it's really very simple – *follow the entrepreneur*.

I meet hundreds of entrepreneurs monthly. Whether in the den on the BBC's *Online Dragon's Den* or at Ariadne Capital or at hundreds of conferences I attend each year, I see entrepreneurs frequently obsessing about the money. They can't imagine:

➤ that they can do half as much as they can with small amounts of capital;

➤ that they can get going without big money;

➤ that it's a privilege to use other people's money to grow their business.

The truth is that one of the things I look for when assessing an entrepreneur is what they have done already, without the benefit of other people's money.

➤ Have they found a team which is willing to follow them?

➤ Have they created a beta product, which you can do for small amounts of money?

➤ How many hours a week are they working?

> The teams at Launch 48 will spend £500 & pizza building an application over the weekend. During Start-up Weekend, none of the teams felt they needed more than £20,000 max to take their products to market, and for more of them, it was £5,000 to fund the product development.

➤ Have they done informal market research?

➤ Have they trialled every other like product out there to get a sense of what exists in the market?

➤ Do they know what they would do if they had half of the money they are asking for?

Far from being a right, *having the use of someone else's money to build your business is a luxury.* Never take it for granted. Most people have to use their own, or make their own money to build their businesses. If you're a financier, assessing how much blood, sweat and treasure has been invested in a venture by the founder is one of the best ways to see whether the entrepreneur will stick with it when the going gets tough. I always ask entrepreneurs I'm seriously considering backing what percentage of their net worth they've invested in the business so far.

I had little money when I left for Paris in 1988. Similarly, I had only a £35,000 bonus cheque from New Media Investors (for my work on the lastminute. com and WGSN deals), which became the seed capital for First Tuesday. I knew that when it was gone, we had to be funded by a venture capital organisation, or else.

Starting your own business can be terrifying.

At the beginning of Ariadne Capital, I put the initial £500,000 of cash in. Spending your own money makes you incredibly focused and disciplined. It's human nature that you simply don't spend other people's money like you would your own. Unless you have invested cash as equity into a venture and thus have a stake in the outcome – *skin in the game* – you don't really give 100 per cent.

You may only have £1,000 that you can scrape together from your savings and your family. You have to believe – no matter where you start – that the money will find you. The past twenty-three years have proven that to me again and again. And I see it everywhere in my life.

In 2003 Tim Draper, one of the leading Silicon Valley venture capitalists, asked Howard Hartenbaum, who was scouting for deals for Draper Richards, to 'find out what happened to the guy who was behind Kazaa' – the illegal file-sharing service in the music industry which had been a sensation. Tim thought that the pirate who was obsessed with disrupting the music industry with peer-to-peer downloads could probably shake up another industry or two. And sure enough, Niklas Zennström was busy cooking up Skype. Waiting for the capital to find him.

Or another example:

I went to Doha, Qatar in 2009 to speak at the launch of QFinance and a CNBC event. Looking out at the sea of financiers, bankers and sheikhs, I decided *not* to adapt my message. I wouldn't try to be like them. I would just be an entrepreneur and talk about being one. I spoke about how the GCC and larger MENA region would develop over the next decade by entrepreneurs and industrialists. How capital follows ideas and the people who execute them. At the time, I do admit to feeling that I was talking about apples in the land of pears. I thought: 'What the heck, Julie, it's what you believe, so don't worry if that message falls on deaf ears. There's so much money here in Qatar that I'm sure your ideas on entrepreneurship will sound positively quaint.'

Just after the panel, I was approached by the head of one of the major accounting firms who said, 'I think there's someone you should meet. I think you would get along with her well. She's setting up a "bank for entrepreneurs", but doesn't have the connections and expertise you have in the world of innovation.' Thus was born an important investment partner for my firm Ariadne Capital. I couldn't possibly have met the Qatari unless I shared what I believed and how I believe the world should work when it wasn't obvious to do so.

Breakthrough people – Davids – are able to identify, refine, massage, articulate and share their ideas – and they are obsessed with doing so. They can't stop themselves. They glow with their idea. And once they start to develop it, once the snowball starts to roll and pick up speed, other people inevitably notice. The money might come from a government, a partner, a client or a venture capitalist. But if the idea is good, it *will* come.

Undercapitalised businesses never succeed, so I'm not advocating that new companies should be starved of capital. Money, however, will always seek out the best ideas. It flows like water to where it can secure the best return. We have a lot of capital in the UK. If investors really believed that they would get the best return by backing entrepreneurs, there would be no funding gap for young UK businesses. But I don't think of this as market failure so much as a failure to communicate the immense potential of these entrepreneurs' ideas. They are affecting all of business today (see Chapter 4 for 'David and Goliath Must Dance'). Investors need to be told how the ideas will be executed in practice and convinced that they will see a return on their investments. The media is crucial here. It should be playing a supporting role, as opposed to its frequently cynical role. Then the money would flow much more freely to many of the great entrepreneurial ventures we have in the UK.

40

Some of the best entrepreneurs I have worked with looked positively bedraggled when I first met them:

➤ They didn't look as if they would have any sort of impact in their chosen industry, let alone change the world and make a fortune (for themselves and their investors).

➤ One didn't want to be the CEO of his own firm, such was his lack of faith in his own ability.

➤ Another had no idea what his business might be worth. He hoped to sell it for $15 million one day. Eventually, it fetched $60 million.

➤ Many had almost gone bust on numerous occasions. The founders of Rovio, who came up with the worldwide sensation, 'Angry Birds', have admitted to *four* near-death experiences before hitting it big.

➤ Most are pretty honest about the role that timing, luck and friendly advice have played in their success ... at least after a glass of wine or two.

But they all had terrific ideas, so it was worth taking a chance on them. Only a small number of people have the ability to build a game-changer. But many have the ability to create a vibrant business, if they are given the necessary backing.

What I know for certain is that capital follows ideas and those who communicate and execute them. Always has; always will.

41

> All businesses really are ideas in action.

> Communicate your ideas clearly in order to attract capital.

> There have been entrepreneurs throughout history – just called other names.

> Don't focus on the money in order to secure the money.

> If you're in finance, seek out the industrialists that inspire you.

> Advance your business without the use of other people's money.

> The direction of travel must be: money to you; not you to the money.

> Don't let the bastards get you down.

> **STAND OUT, DON'T FIT IN – HELP THE MONEY FIND YOU**

CHAPTER 2

ENTREPRENEURS BACKING ENTREPRENEURS

These days, most people know me as a venture capitalist. But in my heart, I'm really a spy for the other side.

I've been involved with the remarkable trajectories of start-ups like BeatThatQuote, Espotting, First Tuesday, lastminute.com, Monitise, Skype, SoundOut, SpinVox, WGSN and Zopa – a series of companies whose growth has been explosive. Nothing beats the high you get when you see a company take off like a rocket, accelerate through the stratosphere, and finally settle into a stable, profitable orbit in its home market. Nothing beats the taste of success.

Nothing.

Why do people who have made money go back into the 'burning building' of building more companies to make more? Because it has little to do with money. True, money is one way you keep score. And I don't doubt it dominates some people's minds more than others'. But success is a drug. *Start-up success is an outright addiction.*

A new global entrepreneurship model has emerged. In some respects, it's making the traditional job of the venture capitalist obsolete.

➤ Today, companies are being created that are fast, flexible, cheap and operate in a distributed model.

➤ Products are iterated in a constant state of experimentation and real-time consumer feedback.

➤ Technology has become standardised and works like components that can be pulled off a shelf today.

In 1998, I helped the founders of lastminute.com[1] raise £6 million for their first round of funding. Today, you would get a similar company up and running for under £250,000. That's less than 5 per cent of the cost to get to the same stage. So capital clearly is no longer the differentiator between success and failure.

This new global entrepreneurship model will drive a new financing model. Something similar built Silicon Valley

---

1   lastminute.com was one of the first UK companies to exploit the opportunities provided by the internet and went on to be an iconic success story in the early years of the dot-com boom.

in the seventies and eighties. I call it the 'Supernova effect'. As each David builds his business and makes money – whether simply by accumulating profit from his company, by cashing in and selling that company, or by going public – he starts to back other Davids. This model of 'entrepreneurs backing entrepreneurs' grows exponentially as more have money to seed the next batch.

|||||||||||||||||||||||||||||||||||||||||||||||||||||||||||||||||||||||||||||||||||||||||||||||||||||||||||||

Pete Flint, an early member of the hugely successful lastminute.com team, has gone on to build and run Trulia, one of the United States' leading online real estate services.

Entrepreneurs are naturally inclined to help other entrepreneurs. David never really stops being David. Once he has made his own fortune, he tends to be inspired to back others. Frequently, he can't stop himself. He knows that the line between success and failure is very fine indeed, and remembers the help that *he* received along the way. Most Davids are more than willing to send the lift down to the next generation who are struggling to reach the next floor.

I arrived in the UK on 24 July 1998. I had just completed my MBA at INSEAD, and I crossed the Channel to start a new job at NewMedia Investors (now Spark Ventures). Tom Teichman, the chairman, a former Credit Suisse investment banker, had recruited me himself. I ended up in NewMedia's investment business as an assistant director with a modest salary, but with the promise of attractive bonuses for getting deals done. Tom asked me to trust him on the bonus issue when I asked for more clarity, so I did. As it turned out, I suspect I made more money over the next two years than any of my classmates at INSEAD (but who's counting?).

My instinct told me to get in at the ground floor of an opportunity, and grow with it. At that time, few people appreciated the full potential of the disruptive technology known as the World Wide Web. Moreover, NewMedia Investors was a little-known investment boutique. Looking back, I can see now that my decision to take a different path to that chosen by my INSEAD classmates, avoiding the status quo of more traditional jobs and industries, was the first step in gaining my entrepreneurship credentials. I was investing in myself, betting that I could play a big role in the emerging internet industry by joining a small firm and helping it grow. That decision proved to be the best one I could have made, although not entirely for the reasons I had imagined.

When I arrived, NewMedia Investors was little more than three men and a phone. We had an office next to Annabel's, a posh nightclub on Berkeley Square, London. Although the Mayfair address could scarcely have been better, the building was decrepit, and every once in a while the keys to the front door simply wouldn't work. Finding yourself locked out, you'd have to go around the corner to the Paisley Tyler private members' club, head down to the basement and then take the lift into our building. Everyone else in the office seemed to find this a completely normal way to deal with a lazy front door. On another occasion, I had just gone to the loo when I heard a loud crash. I returned to the office to see the ceiling had collapsed. It was not a propitious start, and I sometimes wondered what I was doing there. And yet, I loved the way that Tom operated. He was a total gut-instinct kind of guy, and I was flattered that, as he had hired me, his gut must have told him that I had promise.

I subsequently learned that Tom had been a rather conservative banker before he founded NewMedia. It might have been driven by Tom's mid-life crisis, but somehow the whole environment at NewMedia fitted with the brave new world of the internet. Tom threw me in at the deep end and assigned me to handling such deals as lastminute.com (sold to Travelocity), WGSN (sold to EMAP) and ArcCores – all of which made considerable money for investors. He gave me real responsibility almost from day one, but even more importantly I knew that he liked working with strong women and wanted to build an environment where they could succeed.

Relishing my new life in London and caught up in the whole internet explosion, I started to bring all sorts of new start-ups into the office. I would present them to Tom like a cat dragging in dead mice – showing off yet another deal that I was convinced we simply had to pursue. I was always indignant whenever Tom said 'no'. But for all of his enthusiasm and his willingness to take a punt on new ventures, Tom was not reckless. He had been an early backer of Brent Hoberman and Martha Lane Fox, and was an adviser to them during lastminute.com's IPO. This was long before they became media darlings, but it was clear to see that they had star power and vision. Finally, Tom was able to get through to me by using them as an example: 'Brent and Martha are the standard. When you meet entrepreneurs of their calibre, then I'm listening.'

He was right. The quality of the entrepreneur is everything. In early-stage investing, you are only backing the ability of that man or woman to make good judgement calls. The market reacts to what the business is trying to achieve, and it all happens very fast. You can't run a start-up by a committee or a board. You can't invent a piece of technology so good that it sells itself. You find an individual or a small group and give them enough money to take their product to market and execute their core operating idea or hypothesis. But those individuals and groups are rare and exceptional people.

Most of the venture capital community goes about their job of backing entrepreneurs at an early stage by focusing on technology, market analysis, what their competitors are investing in and the academic pedigree of the entrepreneur. They study market sectors, produce dozens of spreadsheets and carry out extensive due diligence on the technology. But, fundamentally, it all comes back down to the entrepreneurs and the steel – or lack of it – that they have within them. That is more than 80 per cent of what creates success. A successful entrepreneur has to keep going even when he or she comes under heavy fire. They cannot express their own doubts, cannot allow their spirits to flag, in front of anyone. They must be able to convince potential investors to back them and customers to buy their products before there is much evidence to support their claims. The qualities of leadership, salesmanship and persistence make or break most entrepreneurial ventures. Occasionally, something else might be the deciding factor, but usually success can be traced back to an indefatigable leader at the core of the business. These people are not necessarily smarter than everyone else. They simply have the ability to keep going when most people would throw in the towel. When their backs are against the wall, they can be at their finest.

I had been in the UK for just over two months when I founded First Tuesday. Brent Hoberman, whom I met through an INSEAD friend, and I met at a coffee shop near South Kensington on Easter weekend 1998. He introduced me to my co-founders, with whom I set up the first networking event for internet entrepreneurs at the Alphabet Bar in Soho on the first Tuesday of October 1998. Over the next few months, it quickly became *the* place for those with money to meet those with ideas – an environment for sharing and learning what was happening, and would soon be happening, in the world of the web.

I continued to work at NewMedia while organising First Tuesday events on the side, but by the spring of 1999 this 'sideline' was front and centre in my life. Over the next year, I decided to leave my job at NewMedia and take First Tuesday international by expanding across Europe. I had hundreds – possibly thousands – of conversations with venture capitalists throughout the continent. What surprised me was how few of them had been entrepreneurs or built businesses themselves, and how negative they were about those who were attempting to do just that in Europe at the time. Statements like 'Early-stage venture capital as an asset class doesn't work in Europe' would roll off their tongues without any introspection as to whether they were part of the problem.

The reality on the ground was rather different to the picture they painted. As I criss-crossed the continent – spending probably 50 per cent of my time out of the UK to meet First Tuesday's 'City Leaders'[2] and entrepreneurs of all stripes – I realised that Europe had an amazing wealth of entrepreneurs. Many of them had done everything they could to bypass the traditional investment community, searching for funding from any other source and stating that they wanted to avoid dealing with venture capitalists if at all possible. I soon realised that the problem did not lie with the entrepreneurs.

The real issue was that the financing of entrepreneurship had not kept pace with the high quality of entrepreneurs in Europe.

As an American who grew up in Silicon Valley, I was familiar with many of the Valley's big names who had built their own businesses before going on to back other entrepreneurs. There was no equivalent of that model in Europe in 1998. However, by December 1999, *Forbes* was already writing that First Tuesday was 'bringing the spirit of Silicon Valley venture capital to Europe'. I was very proud of that. I knew I was on to something because, in London alone, entrepreneurs secured more

---

2   The City Leaders were local internet business people who found me in the summer of 1999 and offered to lead the various cities where we were launching the network.

than $150 million of investment capital at First Tuesday events or through the network. More than ten years later, I still receive emails from people thanking First Tuesday for helping them find their job, their business partner or their funding through one of our events.

Building a company is like working in a hot kitchen with sharp knives, hot oil and tempers fraying. Only those who have gone through all of that themselves can truly understand the pressures faced by an entrepreneur who is trying to get a new venture off the ground. So they are the people who should be investing in start-ups. This model of 'entrepreneurs backing entrepreneurs' was sorely lacking in Europe.

By the late summer of 1999, my First Tuesday co-founders had all decamped to Silicon Valley, which they viewed as the centre of gravity for internet investment. I, however, was convinced that there was a major opportunity to tackle the inefficiency of the European venture capital and entrepreneurial ecosystems and build efficiency into them.

My day job at NewMedia had allowed me to work very closely with some extraordinary entrepreneurs, such as Rob Lewis (of Silicon.com), Jez San (of ArcCores), Julian and Marc Worth (of WGSN) and, of course, Martha and Brent from lastminute.com. As far as I could see, the only way for such high-calibre people to reach their full potential was through a Europe-wide network of entrepreneurs and entrepreneurial investors. Britain was just too small a market for them. Enter the First Tuesday international network, which I launched across Europe on 7 September 1999 with seventeen City Leaders in various locations throughout the continent. Between us, we would help web ventures expand and build pan-European businesses. On launch day, Stephanie Gruner wrote on the front page of the *Wall Street Journal Europe*, 'few Internet-networking organisations, even in Silicon Valley, have taken off like this one'.

By the summer of 2000, when First Tuesday was sold to Yazam for $50 million, I was more convinced than ever that the future of European entrepreneurship financing should lie in the hands of entrepreneurs themselves. Even though First Tuesday had been a success, I had often been frustrated because of some fairly profound differences of opinion with respect to strategy, corporate structure, business values and leadership between me and the other founders. Selling the business at such an early stage of its development rocked me to the core, but it also gave me the freedom to commit wholeheartedly to the model of entrepreneurs backing entrepreneurs.

I started work on the blueprint for my next business, Ariadne Capital, the day after we sold First Tuesday.

53

The idea was to fund the world-class entrepreneurs of Europe. I flew to Malta, sat on a boat with some friends, and let the enormity of the sale of First Tuesday sink in. I did this by sleeping for three days. A friend would wake me up to have a Campari and soda and some dinner, but other than that, I just slept and thought, and tried to re-energise my core.

Over the past eleven years at Ariadne Capital, I have been able to implement many of the ideas I had originally intended to put into practice under the First Tuesday brand – *particularly getting entrepreneurs to back other entrepreneurs in a systematic way*. Some entrepreneurs are able to dash from sector to sector, but pretty much everything I've done has been about facilitating entrepreneurship through aggregating entrepreneurs' capital for the next generation of start-ups. That's my true calling. That's always been the theme; the names of my companies have just been variations on it.

On 8 December 2000, the day I launched Ariadne Capital, the *Industry Standard* (the Bible of the internet set at the time) called it 'The Net's Next Business Model'. I put up the initial £500,000 of seed capital myself, but then invited leading entrepreneurs to become founding investors in the business with me. Some of these were men and women with whom I had already established a close working relationship; others were simply people

I admired. Today, sixty prominent business people and entrepreneurs from four continents are Ariadne Investor Members. Between us, we have funded more than 100 projects, and more than £300 million of capital has gone into Ariadne deals over the past decade. We have worked with seven explosive-growth companies and sold our portfolio businesses to some of the biggest companies in the world.

Today, many investment houses look for ways to invest entrepreneurs' capital, but Ariadne was the first to pioneer the 'entrepreneurs backing entrepreneurs' model in Europe at an institutional level. And our network of investors is still the only global partnership of entrepreneurs to form the very heart of a private equity firm. It is embedded in the DNA and corporate architecture of our business.

I frequently say that we've built our business by helping 'nobodies' become 'somebodies'. That's not meant to sound condescending. We start with people who are unknown but whip smart – global leaders in the making. And we stand shoulder to shoulder with them as they develop their businesses.

What does all of this mean for you? You might not see yourself as a potential global leader, but the people who do – the Davids of Entrepreneur Country – have much to teach us. As the world grew darker during the financial crisis, I started to think that more people should visit Entrepreneur Country every day – to get a glimpse of the real economy up close. I built www.entrepreneurcountry. com and have invited everyone to join us there. As we trudged through the debris of the debt-fuelled, uncontrolled finance mess, created by an unaccountable financial and political elite, I realised that:

➢ **Entrepreneur Country is not an option: there is no other place to go.**

➢ **There is no other end game to be played.**

➢ **The train has no other destination.**

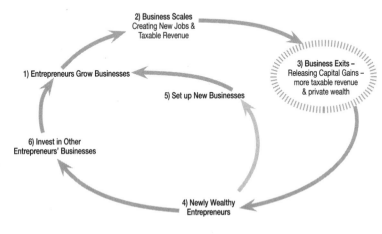

Entrepreneurs Backing Entrepreneurs Creates a Virtuous Circle

Every day in Entrepreneur Country, in the process of entrepreneurs backing and working with other entrepreneurs, you witness the give and take, the friction and the momentum of building businesses that grow the economy. Those who have succeeded back the next generation and give them a much better chance of succeeding – pure and simple. We must do everything we can – at every level – to support and encourage that virtuous circle of growth.

> Entrepreneur Country is being built by entrepreneurs helping other entrepreneurs.

> The main indicators of success for a new firm are the persistence, salesmanship and leadership of the entrepreneur and his/her management team.

> If you want to have an impact in society, don't follow the herd. Look for a ground-floor opportunity that will give you most potential to shape the market.

> Once you've reached the top, send the lift down for others.

CHAPTER 3

BELIEF IS THE NEW CURRENCY

'Never lose your faith and hope. Never give up. Many people thought the rescue was impossible and advised me not to get involved, to keep my distance. I decided to take full responsibility without any political consideration ... We made a commitment to look for the miners as if they were our sons.'

(President Sebastian Pinera of Chile, discussing the rescue of thirty-three miners, 2011)

I played three hours of sports every day throughout high school. My favourite sport was basketball, which I played between the ages of seven and eighteen. South San Francisco High School tended to have strong basketball teams, but I remember one game in particular because we were losing so badly. As the bell sounded to end the first half, I looked at the scoreboard, saw 53 to 5, and felt my heart sink. It would be very hard to come back from this. What was wrong? How had this happened?

At the team huddle, our coach – Mark 'Salty' Sultana – took me aside, looked deep into my eyes, and asked, 'Do you *want* to lose? I know you can play better than this.' From then on, everything he said was about how we were still going to win. Everyone on the team was demoralised, and half our supporters in the bleachers had already walked out. Our losing seemed to be a foregone conclusion, but Salty acted as if I had merely made winning just a bit more difficult to achieve.

His words shook me up. They flipped a switch in my mind and I started to believe. 'It's not over yet. This game can be won. I know we're behind, but we're a good team. Julie, you are a winner. We *will* win.'

And we did. We scored an immediate basket straight from the jump at the start of the second half, then robbed our opponents of every shot for the next twenty minutes. As we hit basket after basket, we started feeling much better. We remembered how our strategy was supposed to work and played some of the best basketball we had ever played. Success bred success; we were on a roll. I felt as if I were in a zone of automatic play. Before too long, the crowd was roaring its approval as we drew ever closer to our opponents. They went absolutely nuts when we won by two points.

I thought long and very hard about that game for many years. I still think about it today, whenever I have a goal that I think may be extremely tough to achieve. *Life is a mental game.* At that basketball match,

I was the same relatively good but by no means great player in the second half as I had been in the first, but I had decided to win at half time. That match gave me an insight into the difference that belief can make, irrespective of talent and circumstance. I promised myself I would never forget it, and I never have.

Belief is a self-fulfilling phenomenon. In my experience, we don't believe that we can achieve the impossible; there is a natural self-policing element to all of our dreams. But most people could achieve much more than they think is possible if they had faith in themselves. Rational analysis and projections on spreadsheets get us only so far.

As a non-Brit living and working in the UK, I can't help but notice how much belief – be it religious or secular, in the form of optimism – is showered with disapproval in this country. Nowadays, the UK is a hyper-rational nation and seems to want to shunt all forms of belief into the drawer. Yet this country's pre-eminent hero is Winston Churchill, a man who believed that Britain could win the Second World War against all the odds. Had he not maintained his belief in himself and his country, the Americans would certainly not have joined in the fight against Nazi Germany. I always find it odd that this nation was saved by a man with unshakeable belief, yet today the average Brit tends to view any kind of belief with nothing but scorn.

> **'For myself, I am an optimist – it does not seem to be much use being anything else.'**
>
> (Sir Winston Churchill, speech to the Lord Mayor's Banquet, London, 1954)

Great entrepreneurs have a self-fulfilling belief in their products and their business. One of the greatest of them all, Steve Jobs, believed that Apple was uniquely destined to bring great products to life:

> Here's to the crazy ones, the misfits, the rebels, the troublemakers, the round pegs in the square holes ... the ones who see things differently. They're not fond of rules ... You can quote them, disagree with them, glorify or vilify them, but the only thing you can't do is ignore them because they change things ... They push the human race forward, and while some may see them as the crazy ones, we see genius, because the ones who are crazy enough to think that they can change the world are the ones who do.

In 2004, when I first met Alastair Lukies, the CEO of Monitise, he said that 'all' he had to do was get the four biggest banks *and* the four biggest mobile carriers to sign up to his company's technology platform. He said this without a trace of irony, and then set about making it happen. He has publicly itemised the top ten things that people said he wouldn't be able to achieve with Monitise, and has gleefully kept records of the dates when the Monitise team achieved each and every one of them. He now runs a $500 million market capitalisation company.

Also in 2004, when the young team at Skype started to execute their idea for revolutionising the communications industry, you could see belief written all over their faces. They believed in Niklas Zennström's vision, and they believed that the traditional telecoms industry was about to go into freefall. Four of the Ariadne Capital team who worked with Skype in those early stages subsequently became employees of the company. For them, Skype wasn't just a job. It was a mission.

Not everyone is – or even has the potential to be – a 'believer'. But Davids always are. If we want more global leading firms, we have to encourage Davids to believe in themselves, and not laugh at them when they do.

I am an early believer. I'm comfortable in the white spaces before a product or a company is completely fleshed out. The potential of a market opportunity and the strategy for seizing it fascinate me. When you are working with Davids in a sea of sceptics, you see how much they rely on little more than belief in the early days. Day in, day out, they have to deal with the rest of society telling them, 'It can't be done.'

Early believers can be found almost anywhere. They aren't exclusively in start-ups. You will always find champions inside existing companies who not only have a strong radar for the next big thing but are optimistic that they will be a part of it. These people – I call them *intrapreneurs* – are vital for transmitting the 'belief virus' within companies. Whether you are a secretary, a driver, a marketing manager, a CFO or an operations director:

➢ **You can be a believer.**

➢ **You can go to Entrepreneur Country.**

➢ **You can become a David.**

➢ **You can help to create a culture of belief and positivity that generates new opportunities.**

Playing sports taught me the difference between being the best player and being the captain of the team. I knew I wasn't the best player, but I was always the captain. My talent lay in fostering the belief that encourages the most gifted players to join the team and allows them to reach their full potential. You know when you are in the presence of a leader because you feel safe.

Leaders are those people who create the conditions of trust so that great things can happen.

Creating an environment of trust in a company can be exhausting, but it is certainly worth the effort. If belief in a mission separates the great companies from those that are merely trading, then creating an environment of trust helps to deepen that greatness.

As I built the First Tuesday network of City Leaders across Europe over the summer of 1999, we didn't have a long licensing agreement that would protect us from each other. I told everyone who signed up that 'trust was efficient', and that we must trust each other if we were going to achieve something really great. The City Leaders overwhelmingly signed up to this ethos, and created huge followings in their respective cities, with more than 500,000 people attending First Tuesday events every month at the peak. We were able to move as fast as we did and capture the zeitgeist because of the trust we shared.

65

Ever since, 'trust is efficient' has remained my mantra for building great businesses.

David is a pathfinder, and pathfinders attract snipers. But belief strengthens the bonds that bind entrepreneurial teams together and enables them to withstand the attacks as they set about creating the future. Early believers are on a mission to prove their ideas in the market place, whereupon later believers join them. When their missions are finally understood, widely believed and validated, they become accepted as common knowledge. For instance, when Lloyd Dorfman founded Travelex, the idea that you should be able to send money around the world was unfathomable to many people. But Dorfman believed in his concept and worked hard to convince others that it was possible. Today, we all accept international money transfer as a simple fact of life. Because of Dorfman's efforts, we don't have to 'believe' in it any more.

I calculated recently that out of all the major deals I've done in my career, 80 per cent initially met with a 'no'. I had to keep pushing, restating, trying another angle to convert that into a 'yes'. In some cases, I had to move a hostile party to neutral ground before securing a positive answer. If I hadn't genuinely believed that the deals were worth doing, and I was the right person to do them, I could never have converted all of those 'noes' into 'yesses'. I don't engage with any David unless I spot his self-belief and feel that I can share it. When I do, I will fight to the finish for and with him.

If we are serious about systematically building new great businesses, then we have to acknowledge the importance of belief as a key ingredient in business building. If you are serious about your business, measure your own belief quotient, for it is inextricably linked to trust, and together these are the new currencies of the world in which we live.

David's defeat of Goliath is not obvious or predictable. There's no scientific, analytical formula for his victory. He wins because he believes he will win.

Full stop.

> Life is a mental game.

> Believe that you can be successful and the chances are that you will be.

> Wear your optimism like a protective cloak every day.

> Be a resigned optimist if that's the best you can do, but be an optimist.

> Trust is efficient.

CHAPTER 4

DAVID AND GOLIATH MUST DANCE

Over the next decade, the world of business will go through a structural change. Just as the Western world moved from a largely agricultural to an industrial economy in the 1930s and 1940s, today the whole world is moving to a networked, digital economy in a global market place. Increasingly, industries are being driven not by companies, monopolies and regulators but by competing ecosystems. These industries are evolving as the companies within them become software-based, with digital business models at their core. Those who are first to embrace this change will emerge as the winners.

If you look closely, you will see that business – and every other aspect of life – is already dominated by networks:

➤ **More than 800 million people Facebook their lives.**

➤ **LinkedIn went public on 19 May 2011 at a multi-billion-pound valuation. By the beginning of 2012, the market capitalisation had reached $6.8 billion and was still growing. This premium to profits is due to the increasing network orientation of the world.**

> Commerce, from fashion to travel, is now driven by referrals through our personal networks.

> The network-marketing model familiar from Avon and Amway is enjoying a resurgence.

You can no longer think of yourself as a silo, or a sole trader, or a stand-alone business. You are no longer merely selling your product or service to another business or person. You are part of a network. So you need to work out whether you are:

> on the periphery;

> in the centre;

> leveraging the network;

> organising the business model for the network; or

> just a passive node in the network.

When I was running First Tuesday in the late 1990s, I spent a lot of time with leading internet entrepreneurs throughout Europe. I worked hard to understand what they were trying to achieve, helped connect them to capital or talent, and in turn gained insights about how the online world was developing. There was more than a whiff of revolution in the air. Conversations would be positively heady with how this company or that team was going to dethrone the reigning king in a particular sector. Everyone, it seemed, was a technology revolutionary.

With the benefit of hindsight, we can see that the rise of the commercial internet was a similar process to the emergence of the microprocessor in the early 1970s, or even the advent of the printing press in the fifteenth century. As the Venezuelan economist Carlota Pérez has discussed extensively, moments of great change throughout history have been driven by 'disruptive technologies'. We have all lived through one of these moments – the rise of the commercial internet between 1993 and 2000. This was a period when the earth shook and everything seemed to move very fast. There was a feeling that new must be good, and that established businesses would fail because of the advent of this new technology.

'The internet changes everything.'

(John Doerr of Kleiner Perkins, a leading venture capital firm based in Silicon Valley)

New venture capital firms, such as Benchmark Capital, emerged during the dot-com boom to seize investment opportunities, while others, like Draper Fisher, grew global networks. John Doerr called the internet 'the largest legal wealth creation ever'. Entrepreneurs no longer tried to make small, incremental improvements to existing ways of doing business. They built entirely new things.

> Henry Ford once said, 'If I had asked the common man what he wanted, he would have said, "faster horses".' Internet entrepreneurs in the 1990s were the modern equivalents of the man who gave the world new cars, not faster horses.

Following each period of disruptive technology, the social and economic institutions of the establishment soon realise that they must embrace the change that has been occurring all around them. Even though the dot-com bubble burst in 2000 and the world was plunged into financial crisis in 2008, broadband and mobile technologies simply carried on regardless, increasing their penetration into our lives year by year. The turmoil in the markets amounted to no more than a couple of hiccups in the inexorable advance of these new technologies.

Revolutionary change has become an evolutionary social landscape.

If every internet entrepreneur in 1999 was a David, wielding his slingshot and trying to fell Goliath, today

UK Internet Usage				
Year	Users	Population number	Population %	Source
2000	15,400,000	58,789,194	26.2	ITU
2005	35,807,929	59,889,407	59.8	Nielsen/Net Ratings
2007	38,512,837	60,363,602	63.8	Nielsen/Net Ratings
2009	48,755,000	61,113,205	79.8	Nielsen Online
2010	51,442,100	62,348,477	82.5	ITU

the two old enemies must work together. When they dance in harmony, they are able to create high-growth businesses at scale. Innovation can happen in both small *and* big businesses, with its effectiveness dictated largely by management execution. However, while big companies have the scale to implement innovation broadly, they are rarely prepared to 'eat themselves' by disrupting the fundamental business model of the firm.

By 2000, the enterprise software industry had grown to $47.5 billion. But companies started to feel that they were being held hostage by the constant upgrades forced upon them by the software firms. After (very expensive)

73

purchase, enterprise software programs generally still needed heavy tailoring, which meant the buyers were faced with escalating costs. Resentment grew as most of the benefits of the industry's remarkable growth seemed to be accruing to the software firms, rather than their customers. Any of the giant software firms – SAP, Oracle or Microsoft – could have done something about this to keep their customers happy, but they chose not to. Instead, it was left to the entrepreneur, Mark Benioff of Salesforce.com, to devise an alternative. He broke with the past and created a next-generation software company. Benioff's business model released customers from their bondage to constant upgrades and the traditional licensing business model. Salesforce.com users simply pay a monthly fee, and they can get started for less than $100.

It wasn't that Oracle, SAP and Microsoft didn't innovate in the development of their enterprise software suites in the early 2000s. They did. But it took an entrepreneur to move the business model from *owning* a licence to a software program at a cost of hundreds of thousands of pounds to *renting* that software for a fraction of the cost. This allowed many small- and medium-sized businesses to reap the benefits of enterprise software, given that they had hitherto been unable to afford it.

Mark Benioff didn't try to build a faster horse. He built cars and then sold them at a price his customers could afford.

Social and economic institutions are embedding the disruptive technology of the internet into our lives horizontally, rather than vertically. Put another way, in every industry, be it construction and property, energy, entertainment, financial services or healthcare, the best companies are embracing digital business models yielding new revenue streams. The same forces are at work across all industries. The winners in one industry have more in common with winners in other industries, rather than losers in their own. They are inevitably:

➢ software-based;

➢ committed to the digital business model; and

➢ consumer/user, rather than supplier, focused.

Smart mature firms should 'acquire themselves', by which I mean adopt a high-growth, software-based, digital, consumer-centric model before someone else in the market beats them to it. They can do this with the help of 'digital enablers' or 'enabling technologies'. Digital enablers are typically developed by 'digital Davids' – entrepreneurs who fully understand the new networked world in which we live. They are

75

'digital natives'[3] who build applications that:

➢ build profiles of consumer data;

➢ connect multiple stakeholders in a transaction;

➢ enable experience, not just the purchase of goods; and

➢ introduce lower costs and lean operating models to all industries.

Most of these digital enablers run small-scale businesses that they launched with little capital. However, both David the entrepreneur and his digital enabler need scale, which is where Goliaths' asset of distribution becomes critical. The Goliaths – established enterprises such as the post office, the bank, the telecom giant, the high-street retailer, or the healthcare service – will have to embrace these Davids. If they refuse to join the dance, they will be left behind.

In my experience, those who run Goliath businesses know that they need to engage with Davids. They don't know how to manage all of the implications of eating their own firm. While they embrace digital, they are typically nervous about how to manage:

---

3   According to Wikipedia, 'digital natives' were born during or after the general introduction of digital technology. Because they have interacted with digital technology from an early age, they have a greater understanding of its concepts and potential.

➤ their boards of directors;

➤ their share prices;

➤ their channel; and/or

➤ their management teams.

Sometimes a set of controlled experiments can be useful, allowing the Goliath to test a direct-to-consumer model (bypassing an industrial channel) or a managed-service model (renting instead of licensing) without risking the whole business. Sometimes engaging with start-ups, whether through partnerships, investing or acquisitions, helps to expand the NDA base of the firm.

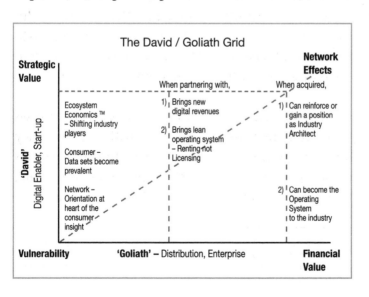

The David / Goliath Grid

We can see these David and Goliath dynamics throughout industry and society today. For instance, Yell, the directories business, which lost more than 10 per cent of its revenue in 2009, acquired Trusted Places for a reported £2 million on 20 May 2010. Trusted Places was a popular, innovative, user-contributed local reviews site. At the time, Yell said that it was acquiring the firm so that, 'for the first time, [we can] enable consumers to recommend a local business through [our] Yell.com website'. The latter already had 2 million listings of its own and 399,000 advertisers. Trusted Places has therefore become the digital enabler to Yell's distribution.

Similarly, British Gas invested £5 million in My Alert, a remote home monitoring and management company based in Cambridge. Obviously the cash injection was helpful for Mary Turner, CEO of My Alert, but much more important was the fact that the deal gave her company access to British Gas's 30 million customers. Turner has now built a £10 million annualised revenue business by exploiting this customer base.

M&A (mergers and acquisitions) activity has always been driven – to a certain extent – by acquiring fast-growing new companies who have built what Goliaths have been unable to build themselves. Multinational pharmaceutical companies regularly acquire small biotech firms for this reason. And over the past thirty years the tech giants of Silicon Valley have played a game of wait and see as entrepreneurs built successful businesses and then threatened to go public on NASDAQ. At the last minute, one of the Goliaths would swoop in and acquire the firm.

Something even bigger is happening today, and there will be more winners and losers than ever before. At its core, capitalism is all about creative destruction, but when there is a sea change – as happened in the transition from the agricultural to the industrial age, and as is happening today in the shift from the industrial to the digital age – new giants emerge that are radically different from yesterday's stalwarts. The business world will be unrecognisable in twenty years' time. This will happen because large enterprises are struggling to understand:

➤ *The new network orientation of business* and the re-engineering of their entire firm that is essential if they are to work within that network. They are no longer able to sell in a linear fashion or impose economics in a hierarchical manner.

➤ *The consumerisation of technology.* In the future, high-growth businesses will all sell to individuals, not to enterprises. People are already buying most of their products and services, even those from business-to-business firms, as individuals first, members of enterprises second.

➤ *The importance of data.* Users' data will continue to be used to fashion and develop new products and services but, crucially, the user will expect either to own their own data (be it their health records, their financial status or their lifestyle choices) or to receive a cut if the use of their data drives a transaction.

High-growth businesses move through five distinct stages of company development:

➤ *Phase 1 – the concept or idea stage.* I call this the 'dinner party stage'. Everybody has an idea for a company, and they share them at Saturday-night dinner parties. I've heard hundreds of these ideas, but most of them never leave the table.

➤ *Phase 2 – product.* This is when you put together a beta product that is more than a prototype or focus group – something you can actually demonstrate. Whether the product takes on will rest on whether your insight into consumer behaviour is correct. And, crucially, today it is *consumer* behaviour that you need to consider, even if you intend to sell to businesses.

➢ *Phase 3 – validation of business model.* This is how you 'tax' the use of the product. It is important that this is separated from the product itself as you could have an exceptional consumer insight and great product design, but don't yet know how to monetise it.

➢ *Phase 4 – scaling.* How do you grow? Scaling at high growth is one of the most common reasons why businesses fail. Everything seems great: the product is flying off the shelves. But the processes relating to scaling haven't been put in place, and then something unexpected happens. Companies can shift into freefall from this phase remarkably quickly. At the dawn of the internet age, working your way through this phase was much more straightforward than it is today. No investor nowadays will give you £30 million to acquire 30 million customers. You'll have to figure out how to scale on the back of clever partnerships (more about this later).

➢ *Phase 5 – sustainability.* Having negotiated the previous four stages to emerge with a thriving business, many people think, 'Right, exit. Time to cash in.' But the goal should always be sustainability, which is defined as cash positive. Once you are sustainable, you have options: you can sell, go public, or simply continue to build the business yourself and accumulate cash. In short, at this point, you can decide whether you want to be a consolidator or consolidated.

Any Goliath sensing that a new industry architect is afoot, or that his industry's business model is changing, has two options:

➤ He could try to re-create the five stages of new company development *internally* by investing in new product development teams.

➤ Or he could monitor the fast-growing firms and decide when and how to partner and/or acquire them as they enter Phase 5.

Ultimately, though, he will have to make a call about his own approach to managing change and risk inside his organisation.

In my experience, Goliaths are more successful when they choose to dance with Davids, rather than try to become Davids themselves. Every Goliath has an asset: his established client base, audience or distribution. By catching the 'digital Davids' early – as they move from late Phase 2 to early Phase 3 – any Goliath can generate high growth. However, if he underestimates the Davids, they sometimes have the capacity to become high growth themselves when they make it through to Phase 5.

Witness LinkedIn. It started with the insight that everyone is always looking for a job, but that you don't necessarily want to advertise yourself on a recruitment board. Instead, LinkedIn's founders came up with the concept of 'passive professional self-marketing', and this idea soon caught fire. Established recruitment industry and media firms could have adopted, promoted, partnered or even acquired LinkedIn at an early stage, thereby extending its reach but also neutralising its threat to their own businesses. If done well, they would have taken some of the economics to provide that reach. But they didn't, and LinkedIn grew its user base independently. It was a small challenger that rapidly became *the* industry giant.

If the established firms had taken it seriously as an industry game-changer or adopted its enabling technology faster themselves, they could have squashed LinkedIn. But they didn't. Perhaps they didn't understand that the world was now network oriented. Perhaps they underestimated a bunch of young entrepreneurs. Perhaps they were simply lazy. But following LinkedIn's IPO, the company has hundreds of millions to continue to develop its platform and market power.

There's no chance of it being squashed or under-estimated now.

LinkedIn was a digital David. Now it's a high-growth David. It really doesn't need any help from the Goliaths any more.

Don't worry if you're not a technologist. And it's OK if you're not a 'disruptive' sort of person. Never forget that innovation is not really about technology; it's about economics. If it were about technology, we'd all be flying around the world on Concorde. Instead, we are all packed into jumbo jets.

Steve Jobs understood this. He and the firm he led, Apple, were game-changers in two industries: music and mobile telecoms. Jobs's ultimate legacy does not rest on the beautiful products his company makes, but on the revolutionary business models he invented. He took on the mobile carrier Goliaths who were thwarting innovation by dominating the economics of the sector. His genius lay in reorganising the business model of the mobile industry through the iPhone and its App Store, with contracts between carriers and Apple that dictated how the economics would be shared in a multi-stakeholder world. With users, developers, device manufacturers and mobile carriers all wanting a share, someone had to change the way the game was played – and that person was Steve Jobs. As a result of incentivising application developers, there's been an explosion of apps for the iPhone since 2006.

Earlier, in a similar fashion, Jobs had opened up the music industry with the iPod, iTunes and a business model that gave everyone involved in the process of listening to music a piece of the action – the artist, the listener, the label and, of course, Apple. Within less than a decade, Apple, rather than the record label giants, was calling the shots in the music industry.

The next big battle in web development will be fought over who owns the economic value of the data you generate whenever you shop, search or live online. Google has become a multi-billion-pound company by aggregating our personal data anonymously and then selling it to advertisers. I may get a great search engine as a result, but I'm certainly not getting my fair share financially. So far, users of the internet have been willing to accept this, but Google has known for some time that the days of its original business model are numbered. The company's leaders knew that Google would struggle to compete as soon as another entrepreneur built a business model that scaled and cut the user in on the economic value of their personal data.

I found that entrepreneur. His name is John Paleomylites.

He set up a price comparison website called BeatThat Quote in 2005, and Ariadne Capital advised him from 2009 until the sale of the firm on 4 March 2011. BeatThatQuote was not considered the industry leader, despite being one of the fastest-growing companies in 2007. However, it had an innovative business model, offering cashback deals to customers, and pretty soon this reshaped the whole online financial services price comparison sector.

The company that purchased BeatThatQuote was Google. The price was £37.7 million. This was remarkable for a number of reasons, but primarily because Google understood that the financial value of BeatThatQuote wasn't the point: it had just £250,000 of EBITDA[4] at the time of the acquisition. But its strategic value as a digital enabler to the immense distribution base that Google provides globally was massive. *BeatThatQuote cut to the heart of Google's business model, which doesn't incentivise the user economically.*

Obongo, set up by my First Tuesday co-founders, was the first start-up to try to help consumers manage their identities online. It was sold to TimeWarner in 2000. Jellyfish, eventually acquired by Microsoft

---

4   Earnings before interest, taxes, depreciation and amortisation.

in 2006, also attempted to use the cashback model. Phorm, a contextual search engine using ISPs to safeguard the user's privacy, is gaining traction after an initial setback. There are always many failures before a breakthrough.

John Paleomylites is a breakthrough entrepreneur who had the vision to see that the game he was playing was one of business model architecture.

The new digital music industry is awash with similarly innovative businesses whose founders share that vision:

➤ Pandora, a company which enables 'music discovery' online, went public in early July 2011 with a billion-dollar-plus valuation.

➤ UK digital music firms, such as Shazam, SoundOut and Omnifone, are redefining the industry by reshaping business models. Now everyone who participates in the creation and/or consumption of great music is cut into the economics of the transaction.

➤ In December 2011 Spotify announced that it was opening up its application to turn it into a platform. This is a calculated attempt of a David to become a Goliath, and it just might work.

Those who restructure industries by designing new business models are winners. If that sounds grandiose, it's not. The whole process invariably starts with a simple 'Why?'

By crowd-sourcing music content, SoundOut has compiled vast vaults of songs that it can access. The company's CEO, David Courtier-Dutton, started with the question: 'Why can't I find music that sounds like other music I like?' The music revolution on the internet has swamped the consumer with average (and below-average) content. As a result, many consumers have retreated to the trusted tastemakers: radio is now more popular than ever. One of the few ways to break an artist is through radio exposure, so the stations are rapidly becoming the new power-brokers – the new Goliaths – in the music industry. Meanwhile, the old Goliaths – the record labels – have persisted in thinking linearly and hierarchically, stubbornly refusing to embrace the new network orientation of the industry.

SoundOut is David to the radio industry Goliaths.

Launched in October 2010, Courtier-Dutton's company is now being used by a majority of the UK's radio stations to identify tracks to include on their playlists. SoundOut provides accurate, predictive insight into any track's potential. This is the first predictive technology the industry has ever had at its disposal. SoundOut is affordable (around twenty pounds) and accessible to all artists around the world. It is fast becoming a crowd-powered filter to enable artists to submit their tracks and get themselves heard by radio stations, record labels, publishers and advertisers.

Recently launched on Radio.com, *Tomorrow's Hits Today* plays consistently excellent music, accurately predicting what will be in the charts in a few weeks' time. Whether you are Lady Gaga or an unknown, unsigned artist, the station only plays tracks that it rates in excess of 80 per cent market potential, courtesy of SoundOut.

Meanwhile, Omnifone, led by Rob Lewis, a serial UK entrepreneur, is another music industry David. It is currently developing an end-to-end streaming music service for consumer electronics, mobile and automotive partners. Omnifone builds, licenses and runs proven, scalable, cloud music services on its MusicStation platform across virtually any connected device type on a white-label and co-branded basis. It removes the development, licensing, time and technology barriers to entry that a Goliath brand would have to overcome to bring a cloud music service to the market. Omnifone's partners already include Sony Ericsson, Telenor Sweden, Vodafone, 3 Hong Kong and Hewlett-Packard. These were all natural allies for Omnifone. If you are to thrive in one of the new digital ecosystems, it is essential to identify such natural allies and convince them that it is in their best interests to help you become successful.

Whether you are a David or a Goliath, you will always have natural allies, but you might well have to put some effort into finding them:

➤ Sometimes they might be operating in adjacent industries.

➤ Sometimes they might be companies that have lost their sparkle, but could be revived with your help.

➤ Sometimes you might have viewed them as competitors, so dismissed working with them in the past, but now a new alignment is possible.

➤ Sometimes they might be doing exactly what you are doing in another ecosystem or industry.

Organising a business model so that it is in the interests of one's natural allies can be termed 'Ecosystem Economics'.[5] As a model for predicting winners and losers, this will drive the next wave of economic growth: not just on the web but across all industries; and not just in the West but around the globe.

---

5   ™ Ariadne Capital.

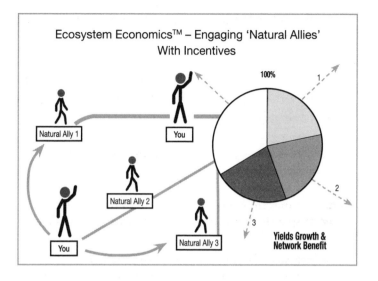

Companies will expand when more people are able to participate and share the economics. Those that refuse to do this will shrink. Every single company that has become or is emerging as a dominant player in recent years has already recognised the underlying logic of Ecosystem Economics. It's just that they don't always refer to what they're doing in those terms. Ecosystem Economics will shift industries and cause new winners and losers to grow and decline faster than anything we've seen over the past century. So how do you implement it?

You simply have to ensure that any new product or service

provided by your company is in the best interests of as many people as possible inside your network.

Monitise became the global leader in mobile banking and payments by working hard to *enable* the mobile carriers and retail banks, not by threatening to disrupt them. The company takes a cut of every transaction but, crucially, it shares the revenue with everyone in the ecosystem who participates in that transaction: typically, the bank, the mobile carrier and the user (in the form of a lower cost of capital). At the time of writing, every twenty seconds someone in the world was using a Monitise service. If you were on the board of directors of Western Union, you might be worried.

Alastair Lukies, Monitise's CEO, has said many times that 'you can't build an ecosystem without humility'. I would add: 'No one does anything that is not in their interest. So make it in their interest to help you succeed.'

In early 2012, Monitise launched the 'Mobile Money' network with the personal backing of Charles Dunstone, the founder of Carphone Warehouse, and Stuart Rose as chairman. Lukies's vision and feats of market grab attracted the attention of VISA, a Goliath in the financial services world. VISA have now invested in Monitise five times, and each time at a premium to what they could have invested in the open market. That's strategic.

Consequently, anyone with a VISA card now has access to Mobile Money. Lukies's vision of mobile banking being the foundation for the coming mobile commerce world therefore looks credible and imminent.

It took a renegade from the corporate world to introduce the construction industry to the concept of Ecosystem Economics. Steve Lewis managed the Partners Program for Microsoft, but he is now running Living PlanIT, a technology firm with a mission of remaking the city as software.

Living PlanIT argues that the construction industry remains the last great bastion of the economy to resist the efficiencies of technology that have reshaped every other sector. Despite being a trillion-pound industry, construction firms have had little incentive to integrate, consolidate or otherwise become more productive. A Harvard Business School case study claimed that the construction industry has actually become 20 per cent *less* productive since the 1960s.

Lewis and his team aim to integrate IT into the fabric of the city by installing hundreds of thousands of sensors that will allow an urban operating system (Urban OS) to deliver intelligent buildings that are constantly optimised to enhance comfort, productivity and environmental sustainability.

93

To achieve this, LivingPlanIT is building an eco-system of partners, including Cisco, Accenture, the UK engineering firm Buro Happold, the project management software company Aconex, and McLaren Electronic Systems (which makes the onboard sensors used in Formula One). In total, the company has signed contracts or is in talks with 300 such partners. These natural allies will fill in the blanks in Living PlanIT's plan to code cities like software, with buildings, sensors and traffic apps all connected through the cloud.

The intelligent city still lies in the future, but thanks to a series of interrelated technologies, we are already living through a radical reinvention of the tools and techniques of reading. Apple's iPad may well be the fastest-selling new technology product in history, and it has done more than anything else to merge book reading and web browsing. Meanwhile, Amazon's Kindle and Odyssey Editions, whose exclusive deal with Amazon for Wylie books will increase the digital royalties for its authors, have also started to shake up the publishing industry. The traditional publishers are being forced to change rapidly as ever more consumers start to read their books on electronic devices rather than paper.

This has led to an opportunity to reorganise the industry's business model, and e-book pricing has already come under scrutiny. For instance, entrepreneurs are devising ways of enabling authors to share their work in serialisation formats that will be sold by the pound.

Publishing, then, is following a familiar pattern: digital Davids and established Goliaths are cooperating to transform an industry at greater speed and more radically than anyone thought possible even a few years ago. The publishing Goliaths that have reacted quickly will survive and even thrive. The others will die.

This reminds me of sitting across from the CEO of a large telecoms firm on a BBC radio programme in 2004 and mentioning Skype. He scoffed when I suggested it would soon be disrupting the trillion-pound telecoms industry. I countered, 'Your industry is in freefall. It is your job to understand from where the grenade has been launched, and to have an idea of what to do about it.'

The commercial internet's arrival in the 1990s disrupted industries around the world in much the same way as the printing press disrupted German industry in the fifteenth century. Both dramatically lowered the costs of distributing goods, ideas and content. With each development in distribution, merchants can reach their audiences more cheaply. If they're smart, they'll share the economics of their ventures in the most inclusive way possible. This gives people an incentive to drive the distribution further. Sometimes the sheer power of the ideas at the core of the company is sufficiently strong to drive the virality. But more often people want to be cut in on the economics of the transaction.

Overall, then, the future is clear for all Goliaths in all industries. If they fail to embrace the network orientation of business, and refuse to cooperate with the digital Davids, they will be run over by them and then slowly drift into insignificance or be forced to do deals at a significant disadvantage. Their deaths may take several years, but they are inevitable. Witness Borders – a bookshop that thought time was on its side. First it outsourced its online business to Amazon; then it brought it back in-house in 2007. But by then it had lost six years' worth of knowledge about how to build digital revenues. Meanwhile, Amazon had incorporated a host of digital enablers and built online communities and social review sites.

By proactively sharing the economics with the Living PlanITs, Omnifones, Monitises and SoundOuts of this world, Goliaths can help to grow the pie so that everyone's share increases. But not every business leader has the courage to shift to the world of Ecosystem Economics while steering the corporate ship.

If you are a Goliath, you must recognise that business

is no longer a zero-sum game. Winning today is about imagining and orchestrating the economic model for your sector. You may feel that running a business is enough work for anyone, but it's no longer an option simply to optimise for profit company-wide, because the world no longer works in a linear way. You must work with your natural allies to create competitive clusters where there is a multiple win for all involved parties. In other words, you must work to optimise profit for *your whole ecosystem*, starting with the core transaction of that ecosystem.

But where do you begin if you are still building a business and having trouble with your 'go to market' strategy?

➤ Find your natural allies in the market.

➤ Whom can you help, and how can they help you?

➤ Think three, four or five moves ahead, not just about your opening move.

➤ Build relationships with the partners now.

➤ Work out why it is in their interests to help you succeed.

➤ Figure out what you can bring to them, then organise your product or service and your company's business model so that they are strongly incentivised to pull you towards success.

The current decade will see all industries – from pharma-ceuticals to shipbuilding – cooperating more with digital enablers. This will have the effect of driving new revenue streams and reducing the cost bases of established firms. Winning companies – be they Davids or Goliaths – will have lean operating models and revenue sharing models where a cut of the transactions they are enabling is part of the overall business model strategy.

Companies that have achieved billion-dollar valuations – such as LinkedIn, Facebook, Groupon, Gilt Group and Pandora – have already broken through to become the new Goliaths: that is, new platforms that are digital, network-oriented and organised so that users can share their products and ideas to the benefit of all.

Growth is the goal. High-growth firms might be established large multinationals or start-ups that move exceptionally fast. We will see ever more Davids hopping on the backs of Goliaths and whipping them to a feverish pace.

If all of this sounds a bit out there, and not relevant to your industry, think again. The future always feels furthest away just before it arrives. If your mind is still focused on 'linear', update your thinking to 'network'. Identify your natural allies. And keep a close eye on your competition; the chances are that they understand Ecosystem Economics, too.

Now, you may be reading this and thinking, 'Yes, I'm a David, and I'm so glad that I left the Goliath where I worked for twenty years. I have no intention of dancing with any Goliath, or working with people in that corporate hell ever again.'

Understood. A lot of people feel that way. If you are one of them, you'll probably have trouble scaling your business, but there's no reason why every company has to aim to become a global leader. There are a whole range of independent, niche firms that achieve success on their own terms on the periphery of industries, be they independent production companies, small-scale book publishers, PR firms, specialist law firms or custom retail outlets. Big and high-growth are not for everyone. Sometimes, though, your niche, specialist, custom business may become extremely relevant to the mainstream – and the Goliaths – anyway. Being ready to have the conversation when they come knocking on your door with a big cheque in their hand is all part of the game. So even if you have no desire to be a game-changer, spend a little time thinking about how your industry *should* operate.

**'It's unbelievable how much you don't know about
the game you've been playing all your life.'**

(Micky Mantle, one of the all-time baseball greats)

A new global business logic is emerging, and its characteristics have come into sharp focus over the past decade. The firms that understand this logic can be start-ups that grow at great speed, such as Monitise and LinkedIn (Davids), or established players that adapt successfully and then grow, like Apple (Goliath remade by David) and ARM. They are defined not by their size or how long they've been in the game but by how fast they're growing and by the way they have adopted appropriate business models for the ecosystems in which they operate.

Whether you are in the energy industry, banking, publishing or any other sector, you will not be able to escape the fact that the next phase of business will revolve around the quality of your business model.

Successful entrepreneurs know how to think big, even when they start small, and move fast. If you can get an entrepreneur into a large company with assets to leverage through an acquisition, or a corporate renegade to tackle an industry from a hyper-growth start-up, you will have an unbeatable proposition.

David and Goliath's dance can occur in a variety of ways:

➤ David can be acquired by Goliath.

➤ David can be a Trojan horse inside Goliath.

➤ David and Goliath can come together as partners to share the economics of digital deals.

➤ Or David can be extremely hostile towards Goliath until Goliath offers him a big cheque and buys him out anyway.

One of the main reasons to acquire a new company is not their additive effect on revenue or profits but because they will change your own company's DNA and enable your business model. The financial value of acquisitions may be small, but their strategic value may be exponential if they are based on digital business models and Ecosystem Economics.

If you are operating inside a large company today, like it or not, you are competing with other entre-preneurs. Size is not a predicator of success; the velocity of your growth coupled with the economics of your ecosystem is.

Fifteen years ago, Steve Jobs returned to a firm that had

previously dismissed him. Apple was on its knees and weeks away from running out of cash. But Jobs had learned huge, important lessons from his experience with the Wintel (Microsoft and Intel) machine and its ability to devise a successful business model for the sector in which it became dominant during the 1980s. No one would have put money on Jobs in 1997 to create a cash machine. Many people had already written the obituary before he set to work. In 2012, Apple had a hundred billion dollars on its balance sheet.

Similarly, the best entrepreneurs I've worked with at Ariadne Capital were all spectacularly underestimated at first: from Niklas Zennström in mid-2003, to Alastair Lukies in 2004, to Christina Domecq in 2005, to Richard Duvall in 2006 etc. When David shows up looking a bit bedraggled (because he's working so hard), it's difficult for Goliaths who sit in comfortable offices and work no more than sixty hours a week to hide their condescension. But David can often turn such underestimation to his advantage and win in the end.

And he does so by playing by his own rules.

The best entrepreneurs have a similar mindset. Size is never a problem for them. They are already convinced that they will achieve success, so then it's just a case of executing the plan. At the heart of this is a belief that their modest size is actually an advantage. Davids' assets have a strategic value and exponential effect compared with the assets of Goliaths because they:

➤ are able to develop digital business models;

➤ possess an understanding of how their industry *should* operate; and

➤ are able to work at much greater speed.

➤ Begin with the end in mind. You start small, but by thinking big and moving fast, you can reach a very interesting place. Keep that end in mind while you are building.

➤ Build your brand as a David who is playing by his own rules. Make your independence and specialism work for you by creating 'pull' into your market place.

➤ Seek out natural allies in the market, and make it in their interest to help you with your goals.

➤ Innovation is about economics. If you are a Goliath, experiment with digital to understand how it will build new revenue streams, lower cost bases and reshape your company.

➤ Think like an industry architect before you have the opportunity to be one and you will increase your chances of becoming one.

CHAPTER 5

INDIVIDUAL CAPITALISM IS THE FORCE FOR THE TWENTY-FIRST CENTURY

Capitalism used to be about empowered authority that didn't necessarily activate the citizenry. The internet has stood that on its head and shifted power to the individual.

Back in the nineties, at Cunningham Communication, I worked in a team that advised senior Motorola executives on their 'go to market' strategy and communications efforts for the Power PC alliance (IBM, Apple and Motorola's venture into RISC microprocessors and MAC clones), which aimed to challenge the Wintel duopoly.

Andy Cunningham, who founded and ran Cunningham Communication, was one of my first role models and mentors. While working at Regis McKenna, she advised Steve Jobs on the launch of the Macintosh personal computer. Like me, she had studied English Literature at a Midwestern university before becoming fascinated by how the technology industry works. She saw it as a series of ideas in motion, each jostling for position, relevance and ascendancy. I've never met anyone who has a better ability to synthesise a new idea, a new claim or a new product into a phrase that immediately illuminates its potential. She was and is a master of her art.

When I was twenty-six years old, Andy taught me that the media are not stupid, so you shouldn't treat them that way. When they first joined us, some of Cunningham's clients would try to get us to convey claims to the media for which they had no supporting evidence. Andy always refused to play that game. From her I learned that PR – or strategic communications, as I came to think of it – was the process of holding a mirror up to the company and communicating what was there … not what you'd like there to be. If the business was making claims it couldn't support, you had to address the lack of evidence rather than just massage the messages.

I was an unusual hire for Cunningham. An important member of the Cunningham team when I joined was Ron Ricci – now global head of positioning at Cisco and someone who could easily have worked in management consulting for McKinsey or Bain – and there were some very smart PR people, too. So I was a wild card for them. I had worked internationally, run my own one-woman consulting firm in Paris, but I had no formal background in communications or marketing.

I made some great friends at Cunningham, including Brett Bullington, a Silicon Valley private investor, Jon 'Ruby' Rubinstein (who later became the chairman of Palm, was a member of the board at Amazon, and co-created the iPod), Les Crudele (a leading semiconductor executive) and, of course, Andy herself (now president of Byte Comunication). But I struggled to be a good corporate animal. At one point, the human resources director called me in for a 'chat' and said, 'You know what your problem is, Julie? You think you work for yourself.' I tried to laugh it off, but deep down I knew she was right. I had never done anything overtly against the rules, but I *did* feel that I was working for myself. I had enjoyed that sort of freedom in Paris for several years, so I found it very difficult to walk into a box – albeit a very fine corporate box – in Boston.

I was fascinated with and aligned to the extremely powerful vision of public relations that Andy and Ron [Ricci] laid out for the firm. Strategic communications, Andy felt, was a boardroom activity. But I couldn't really subordinate my feeling that ultimately I worked for myself although I never shared that feeling with anyone at the time.

107

Also, deep down, a certainty was growing inside of me as I could see that I would build other firms and that to get great people on your team, *you have to give people freedom*. You wanted people who might be able to do it on their own (or at least thought they could), but would hitch up their wagons to yours based on your vision and align themselves with you.

I also realised that I would never be the best PR executive from a technical perspective – just as I was not the best basketball player or corporate financier – but I could be a great team leader. This involves:

➤ creating the condition of trust;

➤ identifying market opportunities;

➤ picking the best team;

➤ analysing data and performance; and

➤ organising the economics so that everyone on the team feels they will achieve more by working together.

A good leader must also understand that she should hire people who are better at their respective areas of expertise than she is. These people will be able to manage themselves, but they should also appreciate the benefits of aligning themselves to the vision of someone who sees and understands a massive market opportunity.

The Individual Capitalist

Thinks of himself as his 'own P&L*'

Creates his own brand

Can be a sole trader, an entrepreneur, a company, or an investor

Understands that first step in any relationship is to build trust and think through others' perspective

*P&L = Profit and Loss Statement

I don't think that anyone under thirty truly believes that they work for anyone any more. Of course, I include in this group those twenty-somethings who work at my firm, Ariadne Capital. I don't hold it against them. How could I be anything other than sympathetic when I remember how I felt when I worked at Cunningham? They think of themselves as their own brand, with their own P&L (profit and loss). They're just waiting for an opportunity to take on the world. They may not call themselves entrepreneurs, but they are certainly individual capitalists.[6]

---

6   An alternative name for individual capitalists is 'free-formers', a term coined by Carlota Pérez, the Venezuelan economist who has inspired much of Ariadne Capital's investment framework.

The unit of trading has shifted from the company to the individual.

This is not just a phenomenon of the younger generation, though. Many older business people – whether by design or accident – have also become individual capitalists. They have left their company and are working from home and through virtual receptions, Skype or serviced offices. They are developing freelance careers and have no intention of working for anyone else ever again. Indeed, Ecademy built a business out of building a community for individual capitalists – 500,000 at its peak. For the growing numbers of white-collar professionals who have escaped the corporate world to be their own boss, Ecademy and other business networks ease them into the concept of working for themselves.

James Caan, formerly a dragon in the BBC's *Dragons' Den*, launched the Hamilton Bradshaw Venture Partnership in 2011. His idea is to offer a franchise to individual capitalists that will enable them to align to his brand and his network for a fee of £25,000, and then build a small business as a Hamilton Bradshaw venture partner. This is pure individual capitalism in action.

The same is true of Avon. Each and every one of its sales representatives is an individual capitalist. They are empowered agents, and many of them are earning six-figure sums by selling cosmetics in the local neighbourhoods.

Of course, Avon has been putting its faith in individual capitalists for decades. Much more recently, in December 2008, NACUE[7] was founded by Victoria Lennox and Matt Smith with a similar ethos. Now led by Hushpreet Dhaliwal, it has 65,000 student and recent graduate members from British universities. A pure grassroots movement, NACUE's mission is to help young entrepreneurs get their ideas off the ground. Its phenomenal growth over the past four years shows that Britain's young people have a strong desire and capacity to build not only their own businesses but a whole entrepreneurial ecosystem. If you ever want to boost your optimism about the future of the UK, hang out with the folks at NACUE. Their passion and leadership abilities make you realise that the positives far outweigh the negatives in Britain's next generation of business leaders. While we may bemoan the one million unemployed youth in 2012, the reality is that we have been asking the wrong question. Rather than: how can we get them employed? Should it not be: how can they create their own jobs? And can they leverage their

---

7   The National Consortium of University Entrepreneurs.

understanding of the digital world inside of corporates? Never before have the tools been so readily available, via the internet, to make one attractive to a potential employer.

I encouraged a good friend of mine, the co-founder of Coffee Republic, Sahar Hashemi, to write a book. She took my advice and called it *Anyone Can Do It*. Sahar has a wonderful Everywoman quality about her, and she is very inspirational, but I don't agree that anyone can do 'it' – at least not if 'it' is defined as building a fast-growing, tech-fuelled business. Creating a Skype or a Monitise or a SpinVox is akin to sailing across the ocean. A great many things could go wrong, so you have to be obsessive, strong and lucky to succeed. However, if 'it' means working for oneself as an individual capitalist, more people will certainly find themselves doing just that. Emma Jones's Enterprise Nation helps these individual capitalists to grow. And while they do so, they will have the freedom of being in charge of their own time. I am constantly encouraging people – and especially women – to take the plunge and create the kind of life that they want for themselves, with the flexibility to achieve all of their goals.

The world of the SME, the sole trader, the individual capitalist is not only here but will drive the world's economic growth in the coming decade.

Particularly in high-growth regions and the West, individuals will increasingly determine the speed at which they run their own lives. Some people will work intensively in their twenties and thirties to amass as much expertise and capital as possible. Thereafter, some of them will continue at the same pace, while others will choose the different rewards of working less. Some will want to work less all of their lives. The rewards will be different, based on the choices made.

At a macro level, the social contract that was erected after the Second World War has already collapsed. It is literally bankrupt, having been unable to withstand the shocks of the financial crisis, and having created almost unserviceable levels of sovereign debt throughout Europe. And because the auditors for the European Commission haven't signed off on the EU's audited accounts for *seventeen years*, we might be even deeper in the red than we fear.

Almost all of the under-thirties, and most individual capitalists, take a dim view of what the government is providing in terms of public services. As a significant proportion of the population start to work for themselves, they'll be much less in favour of high business taxes because it will become a very personal matter for them – not something from which they are shielded as employees. Small-business owners, of

113

which there are already 4.8 million in the UK, will also start demanding return on investment for tax receipts and transparency of expenditure in government:

➤ Why isn't every salary, every expense, and every budget put online for UK citizens to review?

➤ Whom are we hiding this information from and why?

Colly Myers, one of the founders of Symbian, later went on to build a company called Any Question Answered (now known as AQA 63336). A customer texts a question, which is assigned to one of AQA's 500 researchers, who then searches the web and sends back the answer. Myers was able to negotiate an agreement with HMRC not to treat his researchers as employees. This wasn't easy but he managed it, and it was crucial in the growth of his business. In the future, we will see ever more of these new, novel working arrangements as the old, rigid employee–employer structures collapses over the next decades. This will benefit both entrepreneurs like Myers and the millions of individual capitalists who want more freedom in their working lives.

Governments must recognise that this social shift is happening right now. They must resist the urge to reach for familiar but out-of-date models and answers to new phenomena that require fresh thinking.

Currently, the IR35 rule prevents a freelancer working for one firm. But why should that be a problem if it works for both parties?

In 1999, as I criss-crossed the continent with my First Tuesday business card, I encountered hundreds of European entrepreneurs with tremendous ambitions to build great firms. Back then, though, especially in parts of Eastern and Central Europe, there was a feeling that the best way to achieve this was to create a local value-added reseller (VAR) of a US software giant in their part of the world. Their horizons were limited by what was happening at ground zero of the technology world – Silicon Valley.

Today, all of that has changed. The level of ambition has sky-rocketed due to the European 'supernovas' of the last decade, all of which have been led by outstanding *European and UK* entrepreneurs.

One of these, Roman Stanek[8], is a Czech citizen. He built up his first business, NetBeans, and then sold it to Sun Microsystems. Next, he built up Systinet before selling it to Mercury (now Hewlett-Packard). He is currently running GoodData, which is backed by several top

---

8   Stanek is an Ariadne shareholder.

venture funds – Andreesen Horowitz, Fidelity Ventures, O'Reilly Alpha Tech Ventures and General Catalyst.

Similarly, Niklas Zennström and Janus Friis have become European technology entrepreneur royalty. Having disrupted the music industry with Kazaa, they took aim at the telecoms industry and built Skype from scratch into a company that eBay acquired in September 2005 for $2.5 billion. Then, in May 2011, Skype was sold to Microsoft for more than $8 billion.

Each time a supernova happens – in other words, when an industry giant acquires an Autonomy, lastminute. com, a NetBeans or a Skype; or when a Monitise or Qliktech[9] goes public – the people on the team who built the firm taste success. That is usually enough to hook them on building more businesses. They become firm believers that small can grow big, and that a start-up can change the world.

I recently returned to Eastern Europe and was delighted by the optimism of the local entrepreneurs. They all claimed that they would soon be building their own 'Skype', but that didn't mean they were planning to

---

9   Qliktech is a Swedish start-up that floated on NASDAQ and is now valued at over a billion pounds.

replicate Skype. They meant that they would create something as big as Skype in Zagreb or Bratislava.

Europe will be celebrating its own Mark Zuckerberg at some point this decade. There is a young entrepreneur out there somewhere who will spot a massive trend, seize it with both hands, and drive it hard to huge multi-billion-pound financial success.

➢ Will it be twenty-eight-year-old Mark Pearson, who has built MyVoucherCodes into a business with profits of £5 million in a couple of years?

➢ Will it be Peter Janes of shopa.com, who sold his first venture to some Russian investors for multiple millions?

➢ Will it be Emily Cummins, who developed a new type of sustainable refrigerator during her gap year in Namibia and was Barclays 'Woman of the Year'?

➢ Will it be Hushpreet Dhaliwal, who is overseeing NACUE's expansion from university to university in the UK?

➢ Will it be Caroline Plumb, co-founder of the FreshMinds professionals' network, who in ten years has created a very successful group of companies?

➢ Will it be you?

In spite of the successes of these young entrepreneurs

and thousands like them, many people remain sceptical about individual capitalism.

➤ Some view it as only a middle-class phenomenon.

➤ Others believe it is just plain bad for society to encourage people to set up their own businesses because – *horror* – they might fail.

➤ Still others fully understand its power and know that it will overturn the socialist doctrine that 'government will provide'. But rather than embracing that, they are fighting against it. You could call it job security – but for them, not the individual capitalists!

However, none of these sceptics can deny that it is happening. Every month, I speak to people my age who tell me that their kids don't want to work for anyone any more; or that they have a good job but are considering setting up something else on the side. Even people who are desperate for a job are starting to view individual capitalism as a better way to earn money than working for others.

In 2010, the winner of the BBC's *The Apprentice* was Stella English, a woman who had put herself through school as an adult in order to improve her career prospects.

Following her victory in the final show of the series, she spoke passionately about getting to grips with your life, regardless of where you start: 'When you stop blaming others for all of your problems, you start to move forward.' Stella's 'prize' for winning was a one-year contract in Alan Sugar's business. However, she remained an individual capitalist and eventually quit in October 2011, before the year was up, because of her lack of opportunities within the firm. She clearly does not expect someone else to take care of her. She thinks of herself as her own brand and her own P&L.

The World Economic Forum is one of the most elite environments in the world. I've successfully nominated several of my portfolio companies for their Technology Pioneer award, and I was one of their 'Global Leaders for Tomorrow' in 2002. I attended Davos for three years in a row, but I've not gone for several years now, largely because I've started to wonder whether the 2,000 people who do still go actually control the future of business.

119

Meanwhile, in *Capitalism: A Love Story*, Michael Moore talks about Franklin D. Roosevelt's vision for a radically different America in which everyone would be guaranteed a home, a job and universal healthcare. Security secured for each American. Moore laments that Roosevelt's vision didn't come to pass, and then argues that capitalism must be overthrown.

The Davos vision of the world is that the people who count are at the top of the pyramid, while Moore wants those 'top of the pyramid' people to take care of him and everyone else. Neither of them would admit it, but they share the same underlying assumption that people at the bottom have no clue as to how to take care of themselves or design their own futures.

I couldn't disagree more.

The real action is happening at the bottom of the pyramid, not the top.

In early 2011, I shared a platform at *The Economist*'s 'Big Think' seminar with Iqbal Quadir, the founder and director of the Legatum Center for Development and Entrepreneurship at the Massachusetts Institute of Technology, and a founder of GrameenPhone.

His work with GrameenPhone has provided tools of productivity for tens of thousands of Bangladeshis to create income for themselves. Quadir had the foresight to think 'bottom up' by asking how he could enable people to become more productive themselves, without the need to rely on hand-outs from government or international aid agencies.

Business networks like Ecademy (which had 500,000 active members at its peak), Enterprise Nation, the Fredericks Foundation (the largest micro-finance organisation in the UK, founded by Paul Barry-Walsh) and GrameenPhone have genuine transformational power in society. Davos may get most of the media attention, but individual capitalism is already pervading our lives at all levels.

Richard Duvall, a close friend until he tragically died of pancreatic cancer in 2006, launched Egg, the online bank, before researching individual capitalists[10] and subsequently founding Zopa – the world's first lending and borrowing exchange to be based on people-to-people connections. By 2012, Zopa had facilitated more than £200 million of

---

10   Duvall gleaned a lot of knowledge from Carlota Pérez and her 'free-formers' concept.

loans from individuals to other individuals. That's a lot of traditional banking activity that has bypassed the traditional banks and is being conducted by individual capitalists themselves.

This has been made possible by the internet, which has given people the freedom to pursue their personal goals and ambitions outside the corporate bubble. And once you get a taste of that freedom, you never go back to the old model of hierarchical employment. You become acquainted with the leverage you can achieve through the web, not just other people's corporate structures.

➤ The world will look less like Davos in ten years' time ... and more like Entrepreneur Country:

➤ It will be powered by Zopa and Fredericks Foundation capital and loans.

➤ Its citizens will find jobs through LinkedIn.

➤ Monitise will allow them to do all of their banking on their mobile phones.

➤ And they will be living in Living PlanIT cities and buildings.

➤ The most that PR can do for a firm is hold up a mirror to it and reflect it outwards. The process of owning a market position is about listening to the market, and feeding back into the development of the proposition such that you can achieve that market position.

➤ You cannot control people; you can only give them the freedom to follow you.

➤ A new social contract between the individual, business and government is coming into effect.

➤ The unit of business and of trade is now the individual.

➤ More of society will become individual capitalists as they choose or are forced to work for themselves.

CHAPTER 6

THE WORLD IS BECOMING FEMININ

Bob Reiner's *Mad Men* television series has been a tremendous hit and enjoys a cult following. The command-and-control, male-dominated, US-as-super-power environment provides psychological reassurance and certainty.

But it could scarcely be further from the reality on the ground today.

A new kind of power – one that I call 'feminine strength' – is in the ascendancy in 2012. This will soon be understood and internalised by the majority of people around the world by 2020. And those who have it will rise to the top of their domain.

Such people will possess what have traditionally been viewed as 'female' leadership traits, with an aptitude for:

➢ collaboration;

➢ listening and empathy;

➢ building trust;

➤ thinking about the group; and

➤ transparency.

Women are wired in a way that gives them a profound advantage in a world that is built on networks and natural allies, but men can develop feminine strength, too.

Emerging feminine strength, combined with the fact that women have operated without the traditional means of power at their disposal, gives them insight into how to win in Entrepreneur Country.

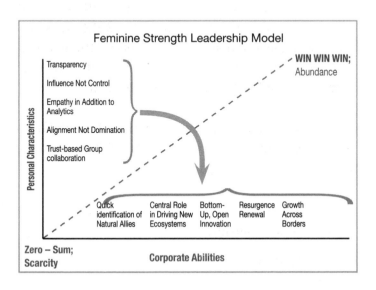

➤ If you're a David building a young company, and you are fighting all of the forces that threaten your firm, you must learn how to build a strategic advantage with meagre resources.

➤ If you aren't resourceful and even subversive, you won't win.

➤ If you don't create trust in your team, they won't follow you.

Leading male intellectuals are publicly starting to highlight women's role in building a better society. For instance, Martin Van Der Weyer, the business editor of the *Spectator*, is one of a number of commentators who believe that the financial crisis would not have happened – or certainly would not have cut so deep – if more women had been making the decisions in the banks' boardrooms. On 26 February 2011, he wrote:

Successful businesswomen may scoff at the proposal of quotas for women in boardrooms – and many men will dismiss it as Euro-correctness gone mad ... But I suggest that anyone who hopes to collect a private pension should welcome the idea, for purely selfish reasons. A report by former trade minister Lord Davies of Abersoch this week was expected to call for 'voluntary targets' to bring the proportion of women directors of FTSE 350 companies up to one in four by 2015, compared to current ratios of one in eight for the top hundred companies and one in 13 for the next 250. The word is that if voluntary action doesn't break the glass ceiling for the ladies, statutory quotas could follow. This means upwards of 600 new senior posts for women over the next four years – matched by 600 middle-aged chaps on the career scrapheap. But male chauvinists who think Davies must have been brainwashed by Harriet Harman and secret agents from Brussels should consider the numerous surveys conducted in recent years that show women to be consistently more successful portfolio investors than men.

Women are more risk-averse, less driven by raw competitive urges, and more likely to stay focused on generating steady returns; and those are precisely the qualities needed in non-executive directors to counterbalance the machismo of thrusting executives. Imagine a Royal Bank of Scotland board made up of the philosopher Baroness Warnock, Dame Maggie Smith in *Downton* mode, the contrarian investment writer Merryn Somerset Webb, and your own mother-in-law ... Then imagine Fred Goodwin telling them: 'I'm going to pay top dollar for a can of worms called ABN Amro, even though we're right at the peak of the market, because I can't bear to be outbid by Barclays.'

The blokes on the real RBS board whooped their approval; women would have told him to stop being silly and go back to his desk. Our major companies, and the pension funds that invest in them, would be a lot safer in the hands of gender-balanced boards. One day, just for equality's sake, we might even have to impose quotas for men.

Generation Y – the under-thirties, the millennials, the Zuckerberg generation, the individual capitalists, or whatever else you care to call them – bear much more of a resemblance to strong, feminine women than they do to Don Draper in *Mad Men*.

If you want to understand future generations or Entrepreneur Country, you must understand women today.

So, how do we accelerate the process of building more feminine strength in society? David knows that you don't win by playing by Goliath's rules. Nor do you win by trying to break through the glass ceiling of someone else's boardroom.

You need to build your own boardroom. Drive your own train. Write your own rules.

I encourage my women friends to become entrepreneurs and individual capitalists at every opportunity. I'm convinced that women will achieve their goals faster by working for themselves, rather than trying to justify themselves and their leadership style to others.

Before meeting the internationally minded students and faculty in Fontainebleau, I had always thought that MBAs took themselves far too seriously. But then, at the age of twenty-three and armed with my GMAT[11] scores, I attended an open day at INSEAD and knew immediately that I wanted to go to business school there. Entry was highly competitive and I knew that I would have only one shot, so I decided to gain as much management experience and international business exposure as I could over the next few years.

Fast forward to the mid-1990s, when I was doing just that at Cunningham Communication in Boston. I knew I was on course to receive a big promotion, but then a female manager blocked it. At that moment, I decided I would never again allow my future to be

---

11   The Graduate Management Admissions Test for entry into business schools.

held so precariously in the hands of someone who could arbitrarily decide whether I should move up the ladder or not. Entirely for her own reasons, this female manager had threatened my future career as well as my entry into INSEAD. Unsurprisingly, I was livid. From then on, I was determined to chart my own course and build my own structures in my career. Relying on the corporate hierarchy was clearly a very false form of security.

Now, in 2012, you have more options than I did in the 1990s. You can easily set yourself up in business, and you can easily project a business façade that seems bigger and more professional than it is in reality. This means that you have a genuine choice between going solo or working within a corporate environment. Hence the rise of the individual capitalists. Organisations like Enterprise Nation, Start-up Britain, or indeed Entrepreneur Country – www.entrepreneurcountry.com – who help people build businesses, are making a huge difference in the UK.

Through my work, I meet a lot of successful businessmen in their fifties. On the whole, I don't think they've given women's leadership an ounce of thought. They would struggle to define 'feminine strength', too. However, when their daughters start to work, they are often put in an interesting situation. On more than one occasion, I've listened to an upset father talking about how his daughter is suffering discrimination in her new job. At that moment, if you're quick and gentle, you can get them to make the short hop to understanding that every woman is someone's daughter. Then, if they are ever going to care, they might finally focus on the equal-opportunity-for-women issue.

I accept that this is a gross generalisation, but I've found that most men tend to operate out of rational self-interest. So anyone who wants the world to be filled with strong, feminine women needs to show men that it's in their interest to raise confident daughters who demand respect and view themselves as their own best investment opportunity. They also need to explain why it's in men's best interest to treat *all* women with respect and fairness. Every man needs to remember that every woman is someone's daughter. If men are convinced that their daughters will benefit from a world where women have equal opportunities, they will join forces voluntarily and proactively to ensure that such a world comes into being. If men believe that they have something to gain rather than lose as the world becomes full of strong women, they will race to build that world with and for women.

The key to unlocking the future of women's potential may

well be through establishing the right relationship with their fathers.

INSEAD's ten-and-a-half-month MBA programme was a turning point in my life and career. It allowed me to take stock of who I was, away from the hustle and bustle of the business world. Sure, I learned corporate finance techniques and organisational behaviour strategy, but I think the most important lesson I learned was that I would become successful by focusing on what distinguished me from my colleagues. Instead of fixing my weaknesses, I learned to play to my strengths. I also learned how to stick up for myself.

I remember a number of occasions when I voiced an opinion in class but received little or no response from either the professor or my classmates. Then, ten minutes later, a male classmate would voice exactly the same opinion – sometimes even using my words – and would be praised for coming up with an amazing new insight. I was perplexed at the time, and even reached the point of wondering if I was imagining it. I would never let anyone get away with something like that today. I might tease my imitator and thank him for echoing my sentiments or simply remind him – very assertively – that I had just said the same thing. I would leave him in no doubt that he was piggybacking on my thinking and claiming my ideas for his own.

But the larger issue was that I allowed myself to believe that there was a 'discount' associated with what I did. I lacked self-confidence, perhaps because I was studying new subjects, or because I was in a foreign country, or because I was in a intense learning environment, or because it was still early in my career. Whatever the reason, I spent a lot of my time in my twenties asking other people for their opinions, rather than trusting my own. As a result, my confidence was weak, which in turn often resulted in my opinions being ignored. I was frustrated about that 'discount', but I didn't realise that I was applying it to myself.

My next lesson would have even greater repercussions for me personally.

First Tuesday, my first venture, enjoyed enormous momentum through the autumn of 1998 and into 1999, such that several venture capitalists offered me millions for a stake in the business. I was also offered opportunities to put together a First Tuesday fund to invest in Europe's start-ups. It was in the spring of 1999 – having witnessed at first hand the challenges faced by the likes of lastminute.com when they tried to scale across Europe – that I decided to take First Tuesday international and create a business out of what had previously been a networking forum. I created the City Leader network over the summer, funding it from the £35,000 bonus cheque I had received from NewMedia for my work on the WGSN and lastminute. com funding rounds.

I knew that hundreds of start-ups wanted to be 'First Tuesday companies' due to the sheer number of entrepreneurs who approached me to ask for funding. I also knew that we had access to deal flow across Europe, were trusted by entrepreneurs, and had an understanding of how to facilitate internet start-ups. My experience helping start-ups grow gave me considerable credibility in building the network for them. A few months later, I felt that there was a unique opportunity to co-invest with investors in deals that were made at First Tuesday 'matchmaking' events – a new service that was launched in early 2000 by Hank Boot. Companies signed up to a 2 per cent fee to be paid to First Tuesday, and some companies wanted to be backed by us so badly that they kept reminding us that we hadn't collected their fee yet!

My vision, my money, my time and my ability to cajole, encourage and reassure the City Leader network across Europe all contributed to making a phenomenal internationalisation happen in record time with little funding between May and September 1999. As it became increasingly obvious that we were on to

134

a winner, I should have made it clear that, as I was giving up my job, putting in my own money, creating the international network, implementing the natural business model and driving the strategy, I should be the CEO of First Tuesday. The market, the media and the City Leaders all assumed that I was. But my co-founders, who by this stage had left the scene to build their businesses in Silicon Valley, were nervous about losing control of First Tuesday. So they brought in an outside manager who had run a spectacles chain as a means to exert remote control from California. (Later, in private, they admitted to me that this had been a serious error.)

I had created a situation where I had all of the account-ability and responsibility but none of the power to implement my strategy and my vision. I still shudder whenever I think about it. And I still beat myself up for not standing up to the co-founders and saying, 'The investors are backing me, it's my money, my strategy and I've created the international network. So I bloody well *will* be the CEO of this business.'

I realised too late that you cannot expect others to hand you a position of power and authority. There comes a moment when you have to stand your ground and seize it for yourself. In 1999, when I first found myself in that moment, I didn't stand my ground. I

135

failed because I hadn't developed the correct muscle. I lacked the steel. All I had was a vague notion that I would be rewarded if I did all the right things. I truly believed that my co-founders would rally behind me and appreciate everything I was doing for the business. Wrong. They did appreciate it later, but only once it was far too late.

First Tuesday brought a tremendous spirit of enterprise and entrepreneurship to the UK and Europe in the early years of the internet age, and business people were forced to think about what it all meant for them. We connected 500,000 people every first Tuesday of every month for twenty-one months. It started the process of creating a new business architecture for the entrepreneurs and investors of Europe.

Started.

However, from a personal perspective, I knew that I had failed to make the most of an opportunity that had huge potential. Losing control of my own company led to a period of deep self-examination during which I learned a great deal about myself. Among other things, I learned that the deal – *any* deal – is always done at the beginning. You can course-correct later, but you can never fundamentally renegotiate the terms of an agreement between people. When I allowed my co-founders to take my work, my strategy, my brand, my time and my money and become equal partners in First Tuesday the business, not just the network which had been an accident, I launched a chain of events from which I would never recover in that iteration.

I refuse to invest in companies that are following a similar path today. Whenever Ariadne Capital, my investment firm, has an opportunity to invest in a firm, the first thing I examine is whether the company has a 'positive architecture': that is, are the people who have invested the founding cash, who are driving the value and taking the risks receiving the lion's share of the rewards? If the answer to that question is 'yes', then I might be interested.

The morning after First Tuesday was sold to Yazam, on 20 July 2000, I met Guy Kawasaki for a late-morning coffee. Guy is a legendary and inspirational figure who at the time was in his own talks with Yazam about a strategic partnership with his firm, Garage.com. Still in a daze, I said hello, sat down and ordered coffee. Guy asked how I was, and I replied, 'Well, First Tuesday was sold yesterday ... for fifty million dollars. I'm still letting it all sink in.' He nearly fell off his chair. I said that I was only just starting to learn some very profound lessons and, more importantly, about how I had messed up my first big opportunity. I was – in a word – sad. I had never been depressed in my life, but I may have come close at that moment.

However, some of what Guy said that day helped me get through it. He is a great post-deal psychologist, and his words will stay with me for ever. He explained that there comes a time in everyone's life when you flip from working incredibly hard for seemingly no reward to working a lot less and receiving credit. He said you always wonder why it hasn't happened sooner! He illustrated this by talking about his time as an evangelist at Apple (a period during which the outside world viewed him as an incredible success), and how, for a variety of reasons, it hadn't been what he had hoped. But that helped him become a very successful investor in Silicon Valley and a leading advocate for the start-up experience.

In the months and years that followed the sale of First Tuesday, I came to realise that my 'discount' had become a 'premium'. First, in my own mind. I had learned the profound consequences of not standing my ground. But I had also seen what I could create. In less than two years, I had built something that investors agreed was worth millions. I had received some credit for what First Tuesday had achieved. I had earned a fortune when the sale had gone through. But I knew only too well that I had fallen a long way short of what I might have achieved. I had latched on to some mighty big trends very early. But when it had really mattered, I had failed to put in place the positive architecture to realise the potential.

I'm a great believer in focusing on the things that you *can* change. You can change the way that you feel about yourself. You can stand your ground when your vision or your achievements are challenged.

I believe that the unique challenge faced by women can be summed up in the road from 'discount' to 'premium'. We have a different way of leading and seizing opportunities. We are more tuned in to the group, less focused on hierarchy. We create trust so that great things can happen. We naturally have more emotional intelligence – a vital skill in a world driven by intellect rather than physical strength. In a network-oriented world, all of these attributes give us an unfair advantage.

We are held back by ourselves. We have to flip the switch in our own minds as to what we are capable of.

Women are good at moving from perceived weakness to strength. Some will achieve much more than their teachers, family and bosses ever expect because they will believe in their own premium when everyone else is still thinking, 'Discount.' They will enter a world that is intimately connected and driven by networks. Their emotional intelligence and innate understanding of how to operate and build businesses in these systems will propel them to the front of the pack. Ultimately, these women will win by refusing to play by the traditional rules of the game. Instead, they will create a new game and write their own rules. Self-belief, hard work and the changing social contract will allow them to move from discount to premium. I only hope that it's an easier and shorter road for them than it was for me.

Not too long ago, I read an article by Jay McInerney (of *Bright Lights, Big City* fame) in which he described how embarrassed he is in front of his eleven-year-old daughter because of all the womanising he's done over the years. He certainly wouldn't want some young man to treat his daughter the same way he treated women in the past.

This got me thinking about the circle of life, and about what loving fathers want for their daughters. I was fortunate because my father is a gentleman and he told me that I could achieve anything I set out to do. I tested that second point on multiple occasions during my childhood by announcing what I planned to do:

Julie would become an astronaut; Julie would become President of the United States. My father never laughed at me.

When a man is a gentleman, his daughters are both blessed and cursed as gentlemen are increasingly rare in the twenty-first century, and the bar is raised so much higher for his daughters then in terms of the men that they can consider making their partners in life. It can be very depressing. But you would never want to trade places.

Growing up, as I mentioned earlier, I was very into sports. Playing three hours of sport a day kept me unbelievably fit and built a psyche of strength and winning that I've not been able to shake to this day. Every father should encourage his daughters to play sport. On top of the benefits mentioned above, girls develop 'body confidence' by diving for volleyballs, swimming laps, shooting baskets and sweating profusely. They learn how to inhabit their bodies.

Years later, at the age of twenty-one, I did some photo-shoots and catwalk modelling in Paris. Suddenly, being a beanstalk seemed to be cool. But girls who should have had unshakeable body confidence because of their looks – far more striking than me – were listless and intimidated once you scratched through the

141

make-up. Despite all the discussion in the media about the thinness of models and the 'obesity epidemic', I always think that both sides miss the point. It's not about too thin or too fat. It is about *how strong*.

Historically, strength in women has always been a tricky subject. Today, we're in the wonderful situation that we can be both strong and feminine. But many people are still unable to accept that. The problem is not just that misogyny exists. It's that so many women are complicit in it. Before you can expect someone else to respect your strength, you must 'own' it yourself. There's no question that a lot of women – as well as men – view confident, independent women as a threat, rather than a social good.

When you look at the facts, however – about how women care for the next generation and are some of the most creditworthy sectors of society in emerging markets (look at the success of the Grameen Bank, built on a business model that prioritises loans to poor women) – you reach the inescapable conclusion that men and women should do everything they can to increase the power of women in the world. And that starts by investing in them.

Returning to the theme of Jay McInerney's article, people slip in and out of so-called 'relationships' very casually these days. My personal opinion is that casual relationships have terrible consequences for women's self-confidence, but a lot of women find this hard to accept. But they are prepared to accept common infidelity and mundane arrangements because many of them stopped believing a long time ago that they will find their perfect match. That's a pity, because we should all strive for amazing relationships – founded on respect, love, trust and passion.

And that is the dance of the twenty-first century that we will watch unfold – how men become gentlemen again, and become wise to the value of having strong women in their lives who are ladies as well as wives, business partners and tennis players.

When girls invest in themselves, they become strong women.

➢ **When men respect that feminine strength, a virtuous circle ensues.**

➢ **Strength and power beget more strength and power.**

➢ **Ultimately, we all win.**

At the moment, though, women still have to contend with a much more vicious circle. The power of peer pressure and poor role models on young women is immense. We need to create an alternative source of inspiration for young women to challenge the media's obsession with looks and whether they are attractive to men. There should be a safe zone for them to be girls who connect with each other as they develop their talents, sense of humour and futures. There should be prizes to aim for, some use of tech to connect them, some involvement from their very busy dads, who probably delegate most of the parenting to their wives at present, and some alternative examples of what constitutes a successful woman. It doesn't have to be Paris Hilton or Britney Spears – no matter how much money they have in the bank.

The new rules of engagement are being written right now by strong, feminine women who are doing amazing things – building families, building companies, building countries.

➤ **Some of us will write that code.**

➤ **Others will merely read it.**

➤ **Still others will frantically try to upgrade their mental software to interpret the writing on the screen.**

This is not going to be easy. Each and every woman is demanding the opportunity to make her unique contribution in the world. And they will want the men in their lives to be gentlemen – strong enough to be happy that they have amazing women to treat well.

You can play this one long or short, messy or clean, but the smart money is on women in the twenty-first century.

➤ Feminine strength is on the rise in both men and women. Successful leaders will exhibit characteristics of collaborative de-risking, building strong relationships and understanding networks. Command and control business environments will yield sub-optimal results.

➤ The millennials and individual capitalists will have more in common with women's leadership styles and feminine strength than they will with *Mad Men*.

➤ The relationship between dad and daughter is important in building confidence in women, and in helping men understand women's full potential in society. When the virtuous circle of dads and daughters is optimised, feminine strength increases in both.

➤ Build your own boardroom; drive your own train; devise your own game; write your own rules.

➤ The journey from discount to premium is always a personal one. Only you can flip the switch in your mind that lets you make that journey.

CHAPTER 7

ECONOMICS IS TRUMPING POLITICS

Every month in Entrepreneur Country, David receives the management accounts from his finance director. Or he may have calculated them himself, or outsourced them to an accounting firm. But once a month, David and his 4.8 million fellow small business owners in the UK force themselves to look at the numbers – often with a stiff drink, a cigarette or a strong coffee – and have to accept that the numbers don't lie.

David can't just print more money if he's short. He can't change the interest rate on his overdraft if it doesn't suit him. His Goliath customers sometimes don't pay on time, but David is unable to penalise them or charge them interest for messing up his cash flow. If he reduces his staff to live within the company's means, an angry employee might take him to an employment tribunal in a bid to get a £65,000 payout. HMRC will demand their National Insurance and PAYE – most likely the largest fixed costs that David has to face every month – irrespective of whether his clients have paid on time or his employees have met their targets. Meanwhile, HMRC seems happy to do deals with large firms that reduce their tax bills by billions of pounds. At least if this is not happening, why are the details of the struck-out deals not made public? It's certainly not in the public interest. David can't realistically set up his business in Ireland, the Cayman Islands or any other low-tax location, if he trades in the UK. Multinationals are able to arbitrage jurisdiction to optimise for tax.

In short, the monthly financial review can be soul-destroying for any David:

➤ **The balance sheet will tell him whether the company is worth anything.**

➤ **The P&L will reflect whether the company is operating sustainably or heading for a near-death experience.**

➤ **And as for the cash flow statement ... Ah yes, the cash flow statement. It shows David whether he is going to have to duck and dive for yet another month. Basically, it tells him whether he'll get any sleep for the next thirty days.**

But a wise David knows a few things:

➤ **Debt is destructive. If you rely on it, you will end up with a less valuable, and probably doomed, business.**

➤ **Don't count your chickens before they hatch. Until the money is in the bank, it's not yours. Payment terms can mean the difference between survival and disaster.**

➤ How to determine whether he can rely on an employee or a firm, or whether he must do it himself to ensure the task gets done properly.

➤ And no one spends other people's money in the same way that they spend their own (although some very good, honest and hard-working people come close).

David drives the train. He is responsible for making sure there's enough fuel, food in the buffet car, and that the engine has been properly maintained. He's frequently caught between receivables not arriving on time and payables demanding money *right now*. He learns to keep up appearances, and how to keep people calm. He absorbs the tension of the system like a sponge, and internalises the back and forth. He may have put up his house as security against the company's overdraft, and his spouse may not always fully appreciate the enormity of the pressure he faces (although many husbands and wives are heroic in their support for their business-owner partner). If there's bad weather, he must ensure that the train still arrives on time. That's his job. He can't blame anything or anyone else if it fails to make it.

Of the 4.8 million small and medium-size businesses in the UK, only approximately 10,000 are defined as fast-growing. As I mentioned in the Introduction, these comprise the vital 6 per cent that create 54 per

149

cent of all new jobs in Britain. These Davids and their firms are the engines of the economy. They are not Plan B; they are Plan A.

But these Davids rarely get on TV, and they don't appear on any government entrepreneurship panel. They wouldn't know what to do with a Dragon if they met one. And they probably never even call themselves 'entrepreneurs'. They just drive their trains, create those jobs and absorb the daily shocks of running their own businesses. They don't have work–life balance. Their pensions are their companies.

Then, once a month, David sits down and looks at the figures. And makes decisions on the basis of them. David is accountable for the simple reason that he has to be.

He has to ask himself a series of very simple questions:

➢ **Are people buying what we sell?**

➢ **Are we charging enough?**

➢ **Is everyone on the team pulling hard in the same direction?**

➢ **Are we fooling ourselves on any aspect of the business?**

➢ **What are the next dozen near-death experiences we might meet and what can I do to avoid them?**

➤ What's coming around the bend in terms of new tech, new processes, new models?

David doesn't take holidays. He checks the company's bank balance daily. He knows every contour of his train's carriages, and anticipates every turn in the track.

There is nothing glamorous about building a business. It's all about those numbers, and making sure that the train stays on the track by doing whatever is necessary.

Young, fast-growing UK firms like MoneyDashboard (whose digital dashboard allows customers to manage their money) and PatientsKnowBest (which helps customers manage their health data) have built their businesses on three fundamental principles:

➤ Your data is yours.

➤ More than that, it has an economic value.

➤ More than that, you will either share in the upside of that value, or you won't share that data in the future.

Why is this important?

Understanding behaviour can only really be understood by analysing the data. Those pesky numbers don't lie.

151

If we could, for example, identify the highest users of emergency rooms, we could focus on treating them more effectively, and reduce their demand for one of the most expensive parts of the NHS. But this isn't being done today.

If you could see how much money you are losing to interest on credit cards or mortgages daily, you might decide to spend or save differently. Most people, however, think only about whether they can pay their bills, not whether they are reducing their indebtedness. Wonga, some would argue, is built around that premise.

Google and Facebook earn billions of pounds off the use of our data – albeit aggregated and anonymous – and share none of the economic value with us. Even a good Goliath doesn't tend to understand data from a consumer's point of view. If they do, they get wrapped up in who owns it and the Data Protection Act.

David knows that

➢ **data doesn't lie,**

➢ **it's yours**

➢ **and it has economic value.**

The European Commission from time to time threatens this company or that company with penalties for the violation of our privacy, but that doesn't even start to compensate us for the economic value that we are leaving on the table.

I would have no issue with my data being used in my neighbourhood to provide cleaner streets, better schools, and safer neighbourhoods, if ...

➢ as a result of recycling, I could pay lower council tax; I would never miss an opportunity to recycle;

➢ as a result of using less gas and electricity, we could have more policemen walking the streets at night; I would religiously turn off my lights, and never wash a half load;

➢ as a result of I, and 500 others in my neighbourhood working at the soup kitchen, shelter or hospital one Saturday afternoon a quarter, I knew that the primary school had a special sports programme they could afford; I would give up my precious Saturday.

...You get the point.

Make it in my interest, and show me how I have a stake in the outcome, and you have my attention. I may give you access to my data and change my behaviour. 153

In early 2012, assessing the ruins of the financial crisis, the role of government and the financiers who have forgotten that their job is to fund genuine enterprise, one might be inclined to ask a very simple question: 'Who serves whom?'

You may also ask yourself:

➤ If capital really does follow ideas, and money flows to where it gets the best return,

➤ if David, who is more accountable and transparent than either big business or government, is creating 54 per cent of the new jobs,

➤ if 'entrepreneurs backing entrepreneurs' is the new model for investment,

➤ if individual capitalism is *the* force for the twenty-first century,

➤ if Goliaths are sitting on large cash reserves, and governments are more or less skint, and

➤ if David and Goliath are dancing through this new world of innovation and digital business models, and creating ecosystems out of yesterday's industries

… then why do we need governments?

In Entrepreneur Country, the role that government has to play is solely as a servant of the people. It must be above reproach, utterly transparent and accountable. It should understand the people's wishes to have a sustainable future where they benefit from whatever they create and empower them to design their own individual futures. In Entrepreneur Country, the role of tax is not to pay for government services. The decision to be taxed is given by the people to government to organise the best environment for the people to live productive lives and build businesses which create necessary and enjoyable products and services. No more, no less.

Gone are the days of deference, when you gave your money to the state and you were more or less certain that they would more or less provide for the populace. The world is being redesigned. A new social contract between David and Goliath; individual capitalists and government; men and women is being drafted. The tablets won't come down from the mountain with Moses. They won't be devised in the halls of Brussels or the chambers of Westminster. They will be written in your neighbourhood, at your temple/church/mosque, within your family, by that new free school down the road, by the private firms, like Circle Partnership, who have assumed control over failing hospitals, and by bloody-minded people with vast reserves of feminine strength who remain convinced that the best days of this country are yet to come. They are being written by the transactions you do, the incentives you pursue, your behaviour, your saving or spending, your decision to work hard or play more.

It takes a special kind of person to look at a mess and say, *'Time to clean up, because what comes next could be really, really interesting.'* But thousands of Davids are saying that today.

This is a bottom-up, grassroots, people-power demand for a system that enables everyone to understand the rules and allows all of them to play a new game. There is simply no reason why we cannot harness a mindset of abundance instead of scarcity.

It should not be confused with 'Occupy St Paul's'. It is not a game of Monopoly. It is not Anger Anonymous. It's time to get out the pencil and the set square: a new blueprint needs to be drawn.

The only legitimate business models – and, yes, I do mean *business* models – for society are those that enable everyone to board the train.

➤ **Some will be drivers right from the start.**

➤ **Others might have responsibility for:**

  • **ticket collection,**

- passing out the teas and coffees,
- maintaining the engine,
- orientating new employees,
- cleaning the loos, or
- buying the fuel.

➤ But eventually some of them will become drivers themselves.

➤ They might have a new idea for a supersonic train, or a greener train, or a train that can carry more passengers.

… You get the point.

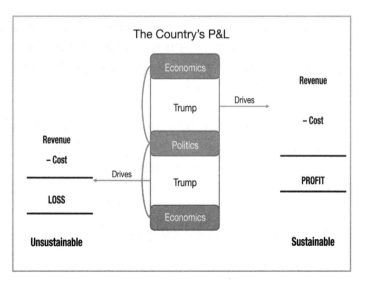

Just like every company, this country has a balance sheet, profit and loss, and a cash flow statement. These numbers don't lie, and we all have a right to know what they are. The individual capitalists are at the forefront of securing that right for everyone. Very soon, every public salary, every expense and every government transaction will be freely available online. When that happens, we will think back to today and ask ourselves, 'Whom were we hiding this information from?'

For this is our money. These are our numbers. This is our train.

Since the end of the Second World War, the British government has been functioning as a kind of feudal landlord. He'll take care of you if you agree to work hard (when you feel like it), but tells you not to worry your pretty little head about how the whole system stays afloat. Today, though, the power is shifting to individuals who want to retain control of their own money and spend, save or invest it as they see fit. In return, these Davids, these individual capitalists, expect much less from the government.

The world is about to get much more unfair unless we build a new social contract. I know from dealing on a daily basis with ultra-HNWIs[12] that by the time they have made £200 million, they have fairly complex structures in place to keep that money from other people's clutches. I also know that those who are building digital businesses are winning twice over. First, they are reaping the rewards of their own businesses and the new digital ecosystems they are creating. But they are also positioning themselves in the new global business elite that is emerging.

I know hundreds of very wealthy entrepreneurs who have made their fortunes and then turned their focus towards solving serious social problems. In fact, I would suggest that 95 per cent of successful entrepreneurs continue to be deeply concerned about the rest of society, even once they have tens of millions in the bank. (Others disagree and say that a quarter of all self-made millionaires are bastards who couldn't care less what happens to anyone else. But that still means a majority have a conscience.) In my experience, those who have made money by building their own businesses (as opposed to being employees of a bank, for example) have a profound understanding of the help that they received along the way. This makes them naturally inclined to help others, but they will be even more willing to do so if there is something in it for them.

---

12   High net-worth individuals.

I have long believed that carrots are much more effective than sticks, and this is more true today than ever before. In a network-oriented world, sticks are almost entirely useless. When dealing with an HNWI, there's no point trying to bully them. Instead, you need to demonstrate why it's in their best interests to:

➤ fund the primary schools of Bristol, or

➤ clean up the housing estates of Brixton, or

➤ create jobs programmes in Bolton, or

➤ work with ex-convicts in Durham, or

➤ travel around the country and teach enterprise societies how to build their businesses, or

➤ fund a new wing in a cancer hospital.

… You get the point.

You might appeal to their patriotism, their guilt, or even their ego (if they fancy seeing their name up in lights on the gates of a new school). By contrast, if you try to hit them with a big stick – say, by increasing their taxes – they'll just run to a good accountant and do whatever it takes to keep most of their money locked in the vault. Everyone loses.

So, rather than moaning that HNWIs don't pay enough tax and casting bitter glances towards their gated communities, we should make them feel welcome. If we want their money – and we do – we must convince them that it's in their best interests to give it to us. And once we've convinced them of that, we might also benefit from the expertise that allowed them to build their multi-million-pound businesses and apply that knowledge to solving society's problems.

Is this our best hope for a new social contract? Frankly, I find elements of it hard to swallow. But those of us who go to Entrepreneur Country understand the difference between Utopia and the real world. *We will build a sustainable world only by engaging the economic forces through alignment of self-interest into a social, common good.* This is hard work because there's a constant temptation to get ideological and extreme. You might not like many of the people you meet in Entrepreneur Country. It's easy to say, 'If I had their money, I'd do so much more good with it.' But that doesn't get us anywhere. The challenge is to create incentives that inspire the ultra-HNWIs – as well as the comfortably well-off – to contribute to the system that has served them so well. Some of them – perhaps 5 per cent, perhaps 25 per cent – will ignore you, no matter what you say. But the rest can be convinced.

In Entrepreneur Country, we have subtly amended the definitions of some familiar terms:

Fair: you get out of life what you put into it; reward for effort.

Equality: there are only discounts and premiums – we apply them to ourselves and either accept or reject those that are imposed on us.

Sustainable: profitable. If you aren't making money, you are either a perpetual supplicant for cash or on your way to becoming bankrupt. There is no global sugar daddy to bail you out.

Individuals: independent beings. You must be independent before you can become interdependent.

Investment: measured by a return quantitatively, not just spending.

Free: nothing is truly free.

Middle class: a status that everyone can achieve with the right behaviour and attitude.

The crux of the matter is this – you can't create wealth as a society without creating rich people. Most are wonderful people, but not all. That reflects humanity, and there's nothing you can do about it.

In early 2012, the coffers are bare. The Western economies' credit ratings are crashing. There is no piñata to crack open. There is only a very interesting, shared challenge.

Can we design a world where it is in everyone's interest to sign up to the new social and economic contract?

Can we agree that:

➤ People who are revenue centres are set loose through much lower taxes and less regulation to grow revenue from which all of society benefits?

➤ Those who are providing public services have to think lean, fresh, local and small, and must inspire and incentivise their communities to participate?

➤ HNWIs should be incentivised to make the biggest social and financial contribution possible?

➤ Politicians should provide security, manage the disagreements, codify the rules that society requests and communicate the new social contract to the nation?

163

> ➤ **Everyone must have a stake in the outcome?**

> ➤ **And no one must be allowed to be a free-rider?**

In order to build a society in which we operate interdependently and harmoniously, we must neutralise the forces which encourage *chosen* dependence or blind *independence*. The enemy of a society that *works* for all is:

> ➤ **government which infantalises the populace,**

> ➤ **bankers or citizens or industrialists who do not care about broader outcomes,**

> ➤ **women or men who haven't 'grown-up' to be independent.**

Successful entrepreneurs always invest at the moment of maximum pessimism. They go out and create a market storm. And those with the best insights into how particular markets are developing are in the eye of the storm. They think differently. They choose to live abnormal lives to bring the future to life. They feel compelled to make stuff happen, often simply because they can't believe it hasn't happened yet – it all seems so obvious to them, even though no one else can see it. Sometimes that blind faith leads to catastrophe, but more often it generates a sea change in how markets and industries operate.

We need our entrepreneurs to organise *now* the design of Entrepreneur Country.

When you live in Entrepreneur Country, you are constantly challenged to:

➤ **Think Big**

➤ **Start Small**

➤ **Move Fast**

Never have those six words been so literal.

CHAPTER 8

DON'T PLAY SMALL

All change first happens at the individual level. The power to reshape society happens when individuals who have decided on change come together, aligned and determined. But to create sustainable interdependence, each person must first be independent.

In the amphitheatres and working groups of INSEAD, at the age of thirty, I started to realise the outstanding talents and abilities of my business school classmates. In many respects, they were much more outstanding than I was. But equally, I started to identify and measure my own strengths. As previously noted:

➢ I was a macro thinker.

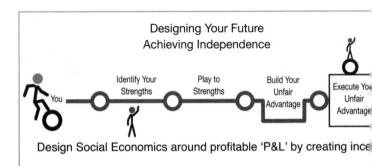

➢ I was used to working in unstructured environments and creating structures that allowed teams to grow (probably through landing in Paris at the age of twenty-one without any connections).

➢ I had hired and fired people from an early age.

➢ I understood the power of communications.

➢ I knew how to build long-term relationships.

I came to appreciate all of these assets by virtue of the benchmarking that you inevitably do when you spend every day with 220 of your peers. (I won't tell you about my weaknesses, but I figured them out, too!)

It's important to understand your strengths and weaknesses because, if you don't, you will be unable to play to those strengths and you'll never achieve independence. Positive things start to happen in a career – and a life – when you build on your strengths rather

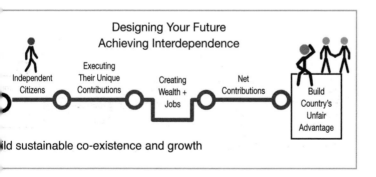

Designing Your Future
Achieving Interdependence

Independent Citizens — Executing Their Unique Contributions — Creating Wealth + Jobs — Net Contributions — Build Country's Unfair Advantage

Build sustainable co-existence and growth

than try to be good at everything, or allow life to carry you where it will. Once I started to internalise and focus on my strengths at INSEAD, I began the process of building my 'unfair advantage'. This was the key to unlocking my future. It also helped me locate my true north.

Other aspects of that 'unfair advantage' grew specifically because of the time I spent at INSEAD, including:

➢ A network of friends all over Europe.

➢ A global perspective (partly because, in those days, before the advent of its Singapore and Abu Dhabi campuses, INSEAD was very Euro-centric).

➢ A consequent appreciation of the potential of a Europe-wide network of entrepreneurs to exploit the tremendous limitless opportunities that were being created by the internet.

➢ And confidence in my own ability to launch just such a network.

I'm pretty sure that if I hadn't enrolled at INSEAD in 1997, I would not have founded First Tuesday the following year. I wouldn't have had the necessary European perspective; I wouldn't have had the contacts; I wouldn't have had the confidence; and I wouldn't have seen the market potential. But I *did* attend INSEAD, so I was able to develop all of those 'unfair advantages'. In turn, they allowed me to visualise the possibilities of an entirely new business network, something unique in the market place, a game-changer: First Tuesday.

So the time I spent at INSEAD was crucial in enabling me to realise my potential. But the process had actually begun several years earlier, when I first landed in Paris in 1988. As a result of making that trip, I

➤ met Pekka Hietala, a professor at INSEAD through my uncle in Palo Alto, which

➤ led me to want to attend INSEAD, which

➤ led me to build my business and management experience over the next few years, which

➤ led INSEAD to accept my application, which

➤ led me to identify and appreciate my strengths, which

➤ led me to develop my unfair advantage, which

➤ led me to found First Tuesday, which

➤ led me to make my first million, which

➤ led me to launch Ariadne Capital, my current business, which

➤ led me to continue to play a role in the financing of entrepreneurship in Europe – working to create the gold standard for Europe's entrepreneurs.

As I hope this timeline makes clear, it's not enough just to gain awareness of your unfair advantage. You must use it wisely. Understanding your unfair advantage should enable you to understand what your *unique contribution* to the world might be.

Ask yourself two questions:

➢ **What are you meant to give to the world?**

➢ **What can you do better than anyone else?**

I believe that *everyone* has the potential to make a unique contribution to the world and make it a better place for all of us ...

➢ **no matter where they come from,**

➢ **no matter how much money they have in their bank account,**

➢ **no matter how many qualifications they have or what language they speak.**

We shouldn't tolerate free-riders who do nothing but take from the rest of society.

170   I believe there are only two types of people:

➤ First, those who think deeply about how they can make the most of their unfair advantage in order to achieve success for themselves. Business school students and bankers tend to be very good at this. Life is a game to them, and they are solely concerned with amassing as many hotels as possible on the Monopoly board. It's zero sum: I win, you lose. And I'll do anything I can to win.

➤ Second, those who challenge themselves to build a better system, irrespective of the environment in which they find themselves. They want a more inclusive world, where it's not about how much you can amass for yourself but about how much you can contribute and build for the benefit of everyone.

I call these two groups 'net takers' and 'net contributors'.

Over the years, I've found that focusing on what you can provide for others, as opposed to what you can get them to do for you, pays dividends for *both of you* in the long run. But you can't be a net contributor for that reason. You have to go into it with the right attitude.

Focus on something bigger than yourself.

For example, when I left INSEAD, I wanted to get into venture capital. That was no easy task at the time, because it was still very much an old boys' club. My tactic at job interviews was to focus on what I could tell London's venture capital firms about the emerging internet scene. I would always begin by reeling off a list of those companies that had just secured funding, before moving on to which entrepreneurs were particularly interesting and why. I ended up with half a dozen job offers because I brought these firms information, rather than merely presented myself as a supplicant. Of course, I was delighted that one of those offers was from NewMedia Investors because it really was my dream job, with the promise of working on a lot of the early internet deals that would be taking place in London in 1998 and 1999. But I got that offer because I focused on what I could do for NewMedia, not what they could do for me. Admittedly, at first, my contribution was very small, but I never undervalued myself – I never let myself believe that I had no contribution to make.

That job at NewMedia meant that I was in the right place at the right time to found First Tuesday. In turn, creating that entrepreneurial network across Europe enabled me to build relationships with thousands of entrepreneurs and investors. Much more importantly, though, it also gave me the opportunity to help thousands of entrepreneurs secure funding, find partners and promote their ventures. First Tuesday was hugely significant for me personally, and its success certainly helped my career. But the role it played in building the ecosystem for Europe's entrepreneurs gave me even greater satisfaction because it helped tens, if not hundreds, of thousands of other people, too.

If you aim to build something bigger than your own career, or your own business, you must be more focused, more hard-working, more committed, more insightful and probably smarter than the rest of the crowd. Think about how you would like the world to work, then figure out what you – and you alone – can do to make that dream come true. Life is about the execution of that contribution. Once you've decided where your true north lies, make sure you look in that direction once a day, keep reconnecting with it. Stay focused on your ultimate goal.

Of course, that can be hard to do. No matter who you are or what you do, you'll have good days and bad days. There will be highs and lows, and sometimes you'll find it hard to focus on anything other than keeping your own head above water. You'll be tempted to leave 'making the world a better place' to someone else – someone with more time on their hands and more money in their bank account.

But there's a problem with that. That's not what leaders do.

Leaders persist in making a contribution beyond making money.

➢ Even when they have no money, they care about more than themselves.

➢ They are resolutely net contributors, confident that they will be able to deliver their unique contribution in the fullness of time.

➢ They believe in more than just money.

As I mentioned back in Chapter 1, I received a very sound piece of advice in my early twenties: don't spend all your time focusing on the money; it will find you. Over the past twenty years, I've learned just how true that is.

➢ The more I focused on developing my unfair advantage, the less I had to worry about money.

➢ The more people I communicated the mission of First Tuesday and Ariadne Capital to, the more money found me and my business.

➢ Focus on game-changing ideas and the execution of those ideas and I guarantee the money will find you, too.

Most of the world loves their own – their own children, their own families, their own companies, their own nations. Most people will do everything in their power to protect their own self-interest. Leaders are different. They have the vision to see that *others'* self-interest is *their* self-interest. They are determined to build Entrepreneur Country through Ecosystem Economics so that ever more people can win.

There is a tension between standing out and fitting in in every environment.

If you are someone who tries to improve, include, create – beyond your self-interest, *you will stand out unbelievably in the world.* Be the change you want to see in the world, but don't expect to have a dozen friends encouraging you along the way.

Changing the world is lonely. Leadership is lonely. Opportunity is lonely.

➤ **Many people told me I'd never get a job in venture capital.**

➤ **Many people said that First Tuesday would never take off.**

➤ **Many people doubted that Ariadne Capital would be successful.**

I could have listened to them, but I listened to myself instead.

If you travel with the pack, and wait until the rest of your class or your family, or the market, or the company, your nation – starts to do something or gives you praise, you will almost always be just that: part of the pack, one of the wolves, in the middle of the bell curve, one of many. No one will criticise you, but no one really will admire you for being – well, part of the pack. And most importantly, the world won't really notice that you came and went.

Silence.

Well, that's it. I have to go. I have a train to catch. I hope to see you later on board.

What? How do you know whether you're a David? Well it took me really until I was thirty-four to be sure...

What's my unique contribution to the world? That's for another conversation ... wink ... but in the meantime, I'm just here to help you get on the train. I've been listening and thinking about some of your questions, comments and interests. I think Carriage 7 would really suit you. They're quite intense, drinking a lot of espresso during the day, and Scotch at night; the plans are big. I'll let them share with you directly. But hop on in Carriage 3 here and walk up. You'll get a feel for the train. There are some pretty mellow people here too.

Got to run. Oh, and one thing you could do for me would be to ... down the line a bit ... start telling your story and sharing your thoughts on boarding the train and how we should build Entrepreneur Country ... www.entrepreneurcountry.com ... you'll be seeing more of it soon, from Newcastle to Truro, from Leeds to Brighton...

➤ Be brave – nothing precious is won without courage.

➤ Build trust – that's what leaders do.

➤ Invest in the success of others.

➤ Play to your strengths.

➤ Identify your unfair advantage.

➤ Focus on ideas that animate you and the money will find you.

➤ Build your unique contribution to the world.

➤ Be a net contributor.

➤ Don't play small.

AN ENTREPRENEUR COUNTRY MANIFESTO

We believe

1 Leaders are those who create trust in society and their businesses, and that trust is efficient. Success is forged through competition. Human greatness is possible precisely because people are not the same and they have the option to choose whether they want to lead or follow.

2 That the entrepreneur creates intellectual and financial wealth through which the entire society benefits and progresses, and so entrepreneurs and their teams should be richly rewarded for taking the risks that they do (and which the rest of society chooses *not* to but from which it still benefits).

3 Government's fundamental role in delivering sustainable employment and economic growth is not as an employer but as the shaper of a healthy environment which fosters and speeds innovation, enabling new industries and markets to emerge.

179

4   Successful entrepreneurs of hyper-growth companies are a subset of entrepreneurs who are a subsector of a strong citizenry who take full accountability for their lives and understand not only their rights but their total responsibilities.

5   That fair and equal access to government and big business procurement processes for SMEs is a key component of a dynamic economy that delivers more real, sustainable wealth creation through entrepreneurship.

6   That successful entrepreneurs cite common factors that shape their unique drive, self-belief and desire to create and contribute at every stage in life – education, travel, opportunities to test what they can do as individuals, learning how to 'sell' early in life, strong teachers, business role models, parents and mentors who honestly encouraged them to be everything they could be. These are areas that we must focus on, providing them to as many young people as possible.

7   That it is still somewhat counter-cultural to be an entrepreneur in the UK and Europe but it is no longer a niche activity or aspiration; the emergence of serial entrepreneurs and the impact of their wealth and experience is felt in their backing of the next generation of entrepreneurs.

8   That early stage venture capital now has two distinct areas – early early stage venture capital, and late early stage venture capital. The only people who do and can do the former exquisitely well are entrepreneurs backing other entrepreneurs.

9   That new, world-leading firms can just as easily come out of the UK and Europe as well as anywhere else in the world. A culture which produces young people who expect success through hard work and their own ingenuity and who believe that they can create the companies which drive new industries must be a top priority for everyone.

10 That the financing of entrepreneurship has not kept pace with the high quality and achievements of entrepreneurs in the UK and Europe, but the capital must back the industrialists of our day.

11 That the triple play of the internet, entrepreneurship, and individual capitalism is an unstoppable force around the world, and that Individual Capitalism is the force that will shape the twenty-first century.

12 That talent flocks to great opportunities, and as those companies grow, leaders should have the flexibility and responsibility to make the right decisions about talent in the firm – not everyone

can or needs to make it from start to finish in a start-up, not even the founders.

13 That great people have great ideas and build great teams, and that capital always backs great people with great ideas who build great teams – always has, and always will.

14 That each one of us has a unique contribution to make to the world. It is our responsibility to determine what that is, and to make it.

15 That we are a small group today in Entrepreneur Country who understand and believe these statements, and that these will dictate the future success of the UK and Europe.

ACKNOWLEDGEMENTS

This book is the first-born, so a long list of people to thank for their contribution to my thinking, my life and my vision.

First of all, thank you to Andreas Campomar at Constable & Robinson and Robert Kirby at United Agents. Boy was I lucky to find you both. Your devoted work on this book, helping me to find my voice and the narrative are so appreciated. Andreas – your editing, organisation of resources, guidance and support have made it all possible and a big adventure.

For the great team at Ariadne Capital, the ACE Fund and Entrepreneur Country with whom I drive the Ariadne train everyday.

For my father, Del Meyer and his wife, Linda, who have always encouraged me to do anything I set my mind to, and to my mother, Lorna Sandberg and her husband, Darrill, who have picked me up when I have fallen down, and listened, and listened and listened.

I have had 3 outstanding bosses in my career:

➤ Robin Lent in Paris in my early days
➤ Andy Cunningham in Boston

➤ Tom Teichman in London

Each has given me guidance and been a mentor in different ways.

And for the guardian angels – Allyson Ockendon, Bob Morton, Mike Alfant, Ian Cormack, Ian Powell, Jalal Bagherli, Nigel Burton, John O'Connell, John Redford, Martin Velasco, Peter Wakeham, Paul Barry-Walsh, Ann Olivarius, Declan Cunningham, Todd Ruppert, Steve Peck, Lorren Wyatt, Peter Bradley, Vikrant Bhargava and Toon Den Heijer – Thank you.

And for the authors, writers and thinkers who have shaped my own:

➤ Martin Luther – 500 years ahead of his time in understanding the power of the individual and social media.

➤ Ayn Rand and Atlas Shrugged – Ariadne Capital is *Atlas Shrugged* in reverse.

➤ Carlota Pérez – a great inspiration to Ecosystem Economics.

➤ Geoff Moore – on how high-growth firms go to market.

➤ Walker Percy – whose Lancelot for me at age twenty introduced me to another great gentleman.

For the entrepreneurs and CEO's that I've been fortunate to see up close and be in their journey – in some small way:

- Alastair Lukies, Monitise
- Christina Domeca and Daniel Doulton, SpinVox
- John Paleomylites, BeatThatQuote
- Jonathan Lakin, Global Dawn
- David Courtier-Dutton, SoundOut
- Niklas Zennstöm, Skype
- Julian and Marc Worth, WGSN
- Brent and Martha, Lastminute.com
- Jez San, Arc Cores
- Richard Duvall, Zopa
- Mikkel Vestergaard, Vestergaard Frandsen

Your vision and drive have been phenomenal to watch and have inspired me in my journey.

From all of the companies that I have worked with over the years, I've learned too much for words - more perhaps from the ones that didn't make it:

1998/1999 – lastminute.com – the first business I helped put together an investment for; the power of personal charisma mach 2 with the Brent and Martha show an unstoppable machine; they worked damn hard.

1998/1999 – WGSN – founders Julian and Marc Worth reshaped an industry with their Bloomberg for the fashion and style industry; they (Julian and Marc with the able assistance of their Financial Director, Nik Millard) were unbelievably clever in how they drove their train to a sale to EMAP in October 2005 for £140 million.

2001 – BeTheDealer – peer-to-peer gambling. Based out of Israel they offered the world's first peer to peer betting product. This was an early sign that the hub/spoke architecture of the IT industry was shifting.

2001/2 – Nanomuscle – Ariadne's first sizeable deal where we raised $15 million into a micro-motor firm in the US with offices in HongKong. Our first brush with large industrial groups investing in enablers.

2002 – Espotting – Pay Per Click Advertising led by Seb Bishop and Daniel Ishag. They had the original business model that Google later adopted. It was acquired for ~$200 million in January 2004. Demonstrated that the UK can build at scale paradigm shift companies, but Espotting struggled to get the funding to enable it to become a global leader.

2003 – Skype – free calls on the web – Howard Hartenbaum, the original angel investor in Skype through the Draper Richards fund, reached out to me in September 2003 asking me to 'take a look'. Ariadne did a lot of the early business development at Skype through 4 dedicated Ariadnites who eventually flipped into Skype. It was amazing to see something go from underfunded to sold for $2.5 billion in less than 2 years.

2003 – Intamac – Remote Home Monitoring and Management – this one hurt. I first met the Founder and CEO through BT, whom we were advising at the time. He had had the vision in 2000 from his work on the engines of aeroplanes while in the airforce that houses would be run like an aeroplane cockpit. I could see it, and I tried really hard to get this company into a leadership position. The company didn't focus on getting consumers using it, but tried and failed to get the telco incumbents to adopt it. We learned what SpinVox later proved – that all B2B companies are ultimately B2C2B companies. I'm proud that Ariadne helped Intamac do the first partnership deal that CISCO through Linksys did with a company in the EMEA region. I'm sad that we couldn't get it over the line. When Barry Maloney, Partner of Benchmark Capital, said to me, 'we were 95 per cent of the way there, Julie' – I had to disengage. It was just too painful.

2004 – Monitise – mobile money. Alastair Lukies, the CEO first reached out to me after a panel discussion in March 2004, and we have been advising Monitise since November 2004 on business development, acquisitions, investor strategy, go to market and marketing. They provide a solution to 250 financial institutions to help them get into the world of mobile money. Monitise sit at the heart of the mobile money ecosystem and organise the traffic flows and business model for the industry. Backed by VISA five times, operating on 4 continents, every 20 seconds someone uses a Monitise service to access their balance, transfer funds, or buy something. Lukies walks on water.

2005 – Zopa – peer to peer lending – Ariadne had been advising Egg and Richard Duvall's team when he and they broke away to set up Zopa. Richard first put me on to Carlota Pérez, whose theory of disruptive technology and adoption is fundamental to my thinking. She also spoke of free-formers – what I would later refer to as Individual Capitalists. Ariadne helped the Zopa founding team with their July 2005 round of capital, bringing in Jonathan Rowland and Tim Draper from our own network. We also helped them secure early lenders. While Zopa today is not the subversive play that Duvall had originally thought up, it is well placed to reshape the world of money. Like everyone who came in contact with Richard, I loved his spirit.

2006 – SpinVox – voice to text – I first met Christina Domecq and Daniel Doulton, the founders of SpinVox, at CarPhone Warehouse where we were doing some work in the summer of 2005. Spinvox would go on to secure £50 million, and be sold to Nuance Technologies. SpinVox were the first company in the world to take the voice to text technology and deliver it as a managed service, and then sell it to thirty-three operators. The leadership of this company created a tight family who were changing the world. I was fortunate to be part of the story.

2006 – Otodio – text to voice – Although Otodio didn't work, they had the idea – opposite of SpinVox – that people would want text read out to them in cars on the way to work, on the train, etc. Otodio was trying to organise a set of actions in a multi-dependency world (a network) – getting adoption by publishers, device manufacturers, auto manufacturers. They didn't have the market power to do this, and they and we didn't focus on the business model enough. This helped us get to our thinking on disruptive economics faster

2006 – Independent IP – a 'linked in' for music publishers. Based in Amsterdam, this management team wanted to start afresh with a way to create the vault of music where rights and income streams for the artist could be managed by a center body, Independent IP. IIP would enable transactions, and organise the business model. Traction was tough as they were dealing with Goliaths in the music industry who were interested in the new new thing, but were never going to break ranks and adopt it. They or their model will become where the music industry moves to. We learned that the entrepreneur understands the new digital network or ecosystem that the established industry is moving into before the established industry does. But we weren't able to help them enough to find their early adopter. We could see though the shape of the David/Goliath battles to come.

2006/7 – Lickerish – redesign of the world of professional photography. The founders of Lickerish had a central thesis around incentivising costs and revenue streams for all of the parties in the transaction. Put another way, the celebrity being shot will choose to take a taxi rather than a limo if the costs of the photoshoot are deducted from the net proceeds to him/her. This was ground-breaking. While ultimately not as successful as they/we would have liked, they were on to a big idea around 'making it in people's interest for you to be successful' early on.

189

2007 – The Bizmo – we were quite captivated by The Bizmo as it was the first time that we actively focused on business model as the disruptive force. The Bizmo had an application that would 'forward distribute' content, and where each party which touched the application would take a cut. While ground-breaking, the application wasn't sufficiently good. The management team have moved on.

2008 – 1click2fame/Global Dawn – the management team was early to understand how competitions online could drive engagement between artists and followers, and brands and users. They have morphed their proposition a number of times, but have successfully built client relationships with Tesco and Pepsi. Ariadne learned a lot through this project – primarily about how the world of TV is moving to the web, how digital applications ('digital enablers' in Ariadne speak) are transforming established companies, and ultimately how it's 'all about the data'. Jonathan Lakin the founder and CEO is a truly remarkable visionary and sales person.

2009 – SliceThePie/ Sound Out – through Paul Brown, a former EIR at Ariadne, we were introduced to David Courtier-Dutton, the Founder and CEO of SoundOut. SoundOut has created a vault of crowd-reviewed tracks from unsigned artists. Through their deal with CBS, Tomorrow's Hits Today, they are proving that it will be the digital enablers which transform the music industry. It wasn't their first product (fan financing – SliceThePie) or their first go to market strategy (discussions with the record labels), but second product and second go to market – speaking to the radio stations who were tired of being told by the record labels what to play, that they got their mojo, and realised that radio stations with a great ability to break new artists could do that in the digital world too.

2010 – Digital Stores – D2C music merchandise –Ariadne advised on the sale to EMI. Russell Coultart did a great job here, and is proving that entrepreneurs with hustle can transform corporates.

2011 – BeatThatQuote – although the sale of BeatThatQuote to Google was completed on 4 March 2011, this was twenty-one months in the making. Ariadne had been advising BTQ on business development activity when they received an approach from Google that we helped to negotiate to a close. The conclusion was a 122 EBITDA multiple on exit valuation. BTQ was a financial services price comparison, but crucially was offering cashback deals where the end users' data was being given an economic upside. We see that data is the next battleground, and that the digital enablers are the ones that are building these consumer data profiles which are then leveraged across the Goliath distribution bases. John Paleomylites the founder and a dear friend is one of the smartest men on the planet.

And for the 'Sisterhood' – those amazing women entrepreneurs who help me play a better game myself and who inspire me with how high they aim:

Sara Murray, Katherine Corich, Lara Morgan, Martha Lane Fox, Judy Piatkus, Elaine Safier, Kate Hersov and Kim Chilman Blair, Hushpreet Dhaliwal, Julia Hobsbawm, Kanya King, Marcelle Speller, Sahar Hashemi, Sally Ernst, Glenda Stone. Michelle Senecal de Fonseca, Karen Paterson, Marjorie Leonidas, Sherry Roberts, Ratna Singh, Christina Domecq, Karima Serageldin and Narda Shirley.

And to my excellent professors at Valparaiso University, Indiana, INSEAD, Fontainebleau as well as the teachers at Faith Lutheran School, Fair Oaks, CA – thank you for helping me think and learn.